ACTSO

CONTENTS

After you've been in ministry for almost a half a century, you would think you've seen it all, contended with every conceivable situation, and developed pat answers for all unfortunate circumstances.

I don't want to disappoint you, but that is simply not the case. There is no template for ministry in times of tragedy, but that means it's all the more important for us to be prepared to reach out and help where we can. We who are believers in Christ should comfort one another as we are encouraged to do in the scriptures: 2 Corinthians 1:3-4 "Praise be to the God and Father of our Lord Jesus Christ, the Father of compassion and the God of all comfort, who comforts us in all our troubles, so that we can comfort those in any trouble with the comfort we ourselves have received from God."

In Acts of God, we provide a realistic depiction of human tragedy and its effect on average people. If you are like me you will be emotionally moved by the stories you see. While the drama should also make you uncomfortable, in the process it should sensitize you to the impact tragedy has on various people living in different circumstances, perhaps not unlike real people in your family, church or neighborhood.

Most of us understandably shy away from these uncomfortable situations, but as Christians we really don't have that option. The good news is that we have the Holy Spirit to guide our actions and tell us what to say. It is also comforting that in most cases you don't have to say anything, you just have to be there and love the people who are suffering.

Bob Russell

INTRODUCTION

An admission from the get-go: this study is heavy lifting!

This study is heavy lifting theologically. The material wrestles with the most haunting question of life: if there is an all-good, all-powerful God, why do we face natural disasters, horrendous famines, ravaging diseases, debilitating birth defects, brutal rapes, massive holocausts, perpetual wars, and epidemic oppression of the poor, just to name a few of the global hardships humanity endures?

This study is also heavy lifting emotionally. In cinematic fashion, the material presents individuals facing infertility, war-induced post-traumatic stress disorder (PTSD), terminal cancer, crushing guilt, and unexpected death, including the death of a child — all in one study!

And this study is heavy lifting relationally. When one person in a group experiences or expresses anguish, fear, confusion, or doubt, the strength of the group's relational bond is tested and stretched. Each person is forced to ask himself or herself, Will I sit with the hurting in their dust and ashes? Will I run away? Will I give pat answers to relieve my own distress? Can I not only rejoice with those who rejoice but also weep with those who weep?

So you may find yourself wondering why in the world your group would take up an intense study like this. But turn the question around. How can your group not choose a curriculum like this? Don't most people, including believers, wrestle with this question of God and suffering, even if they don't talk out loud about it? And if they don't struggle with the question, they surely have family or friends who do.

Sooner or later, don't most people experience at least one, if not multiple, traumatic, overwhelming, bewildering tragedies with which they will be forced to grapple?

To keep our group studies "light and positive," because "that's what we all like," is to deny reality and risk being a superficial, even irresponsible, community of Christ-followers. The Scriptures are not a rose garden of fluffy, breezy passages. Rather, they tell the truth of the real grittiness of existence here on planet earth. From Cain's senseless murder of Abel to Jesus' gruesome execution on the cross, the Bible is filled from one end to the other with honest accounts of calamity and suffering, all told without candy coating. "In this world you will have trouble," Jesus said, so we shouldn't stick our heads in the sand.

Since suffering, and the questions raised by suffering, are all around us, isn't it better to wrestle with these issues head on and in the context of a loving, safe community where we can share each other's stories, sorrows, and discoveries?

This study won't be a walk in the park. It might feel more like a walk through the valley of the shadow of death. But isn't that where we are most likely to find Jesus' rod and staff comforting us, our heads anointed with healing oil, and, at least sometimes, our cups overflowing with a profound joy that the "light and positive" can never produce?

Goals for this study

1. to wrestle together as a community with the meaning of suffering

2. to come to grips with our own suffering and how we cope with it

3. to share our experiences with each other so that together we "bear one another's burdens and so fulfill the law of Christ" (Galatians 6:2, New King James Version)

To meet these goals, this curriculum includes four distinct, yet complimentary, elements:

1. The Teaching Element: In each video, Bob Russell teaches through the life of Joseph as a high water mark of faithfulness during suffering.

2. The Story Element: Also in each video, a story unfolds in which divergent characters face various kinds of distress. There is no one "Joseph" figure in the cinematic content, but each character wrestles with his or her own reaction to their personal anguish.

3. The Journal Element: In response to the teaching and story, participants are challenged to wrestle with their own intellectual and emotional responses to suffering through use of an interactive daily journal.

4. The Community Element: At each gathering, your group is guided to discuss the teaching, reflect on the story, and share their experiences and reactions to suffering.

Expect each one of these elements to be different in feel and emphasis. This diversity reflects the variety we find in Scripture itself, which includes Job as well as Joseph; Ecclesiastes as well as Proverbs, lament Psalms as well as praise Psalms; and Jesus himself commending confident trust in the Father yet weeping with sorrow in the garden.

About this Traveler's Journal

The Traveler's Journal is a companion for this trek through the valley of the shadow. The journal leads you in "Daily Strides" along the journey of dealing with suffering and grief. These bite-sized portions help you slowly chew on and digest the huge issues surrounding suffering, loss, and death that arise in the teaching videos. The insights and experiences from the journal will provide rich material for discussion and increased opportunities for bonding in your group. We hope that the Traveler's Journal will enhance the value of the group experience significantly. If your group is going to wrestle with some of the most gut-wrenching subjects in life, why not go as deep and complete as you can?

Note that the Traveler's Journal is not a typical Bible study workbook where one summaries Scriptures with fill-in-the-blank answers. Rather, the journal is indeed a journal, and a journal is a record of a journey. The journal guides you through a journey of grappling with your own suffering, and your reactions to others' suffering, as well as wrestling with the intellectual problem of pain.

A common question at this point is, I can see why we need to wrestle with the theological problem of pain. But why focus on my own pain and suffering, and how I cope with it? That seems like such a downer. Isn't past suffering better just left in the past?

Maybe, but consider this: When a person avoids thinking about his suffering, the pain doesn't go away. The pain goes underground. The suffering is still having an effect, but this effect is off the radar screen. The person thinks they are choosing how they will respond to suffering - by ignoring it! But in fact some involuntary, automatic, reflexive reaction is occurring beneath the surface of their awareness. It's like a computer program, of which the user is unaware, running in the background. The program is consuming precious resources and affecting the machine's overall performance, but the user is blind to these effects.

For example, whenever Kelly cried as a child or had a hard day, her mom would make her something to eat. Now whenever she is stressed, afraid or sad, she automatically turns to food. Kelly has yet to consciously connect her eating to her pain. But she wonders why she can't stay on a diet or keep weight off after she loses it. In actuality, she has rarely experienced her hurts in any meaningful way because, before she feels pain for any length of time, she has already medicated her pain with food. So while Kelly thinks she doesn't bother with her hurts, this very fact of ignoring her hurts is causing further damage in her life.

Or consider Taylor. His knee-jerk reaction to suffering is to simply ignore it - a reaction subconsciously learned from parents who modeled this response. So for Taylor his pain avoidance is natural and unquestioned. But it is also outside of his awareness. Not only that, but the effects of Taylor's manner of dealing with pain are also outside of conscious awareness.

When someone disconnects from emotions like grief or regret, other emotions get walled off as well. So when Taylor has trouble feeling any emotion deeply – even positive emotions like happiness, hope or sympathy - he might conclude that he is just not an emotional person. All the while, he is unaware that his automatic reaction of shutting down painful emotions has also shut down positive emotions.

Taylor's automatic reaction to suffering not only affects him, but also spills over onto others. When his wife or children experience pain, he isn't able to feel their pain with them. And he will likely expect others to just "get over it" like he does.

Taylor may even characterize his response to suffering as "faithful" because he doesn't let suffering affect him. To him, ignoring pain seems like trusting God. But actually, Taylor has never trusted God with his suffering at all. Ignoring suffering is not the same as trusting God with it. So while Taylor may think his past hardships have little effect on him, the effects are just hidden, and being hidden, are outside of his control.

If we avoid facing our sufferings, we miss out on what they have to teach us.

If we face, and even embrace our pains, we give Jesus a chance to teach us about them, and even heal them.

Tips for the Traveler's Journal:

- Don't feel obligated to do all the Daily Strides. Our lives are busy, so if you miss a day or more, don't beat yourself up. Do what you can.

- The design incorporates a schedule of morning and evening encounters with God and this material. The rationale for this schedule is to encourage one to begin and end the day with God. However, feel free to decide a timetable that works best for you.

- Also, some strides can be emotionally challenging. If an exercise feels like too much, don't feel bad about skipping it. So much depends on where you are in your journey, how many hurts you have, and how fresh your hurts are.

- That being said, push through even when it's difficult; go a little further than you think you can. It's often in that "one-step-further" zone that our greatest growth occurs.

ACTS OF GOD

PREPARATORY SESSION

Daily Strides BEFORE the Preparatory Session

The Daily Strides in this section are groundwork for the group's Preparatory Session. If your group is including this session as part of the study, begin here. (Even if your group is not including the Preparatory Session, you are encouraged to complete these Daily Strides, as they can help you sort out the emotions triggered in this study.)

Since the Acts of God study is intense, intense emotions may arise in you or your fellow group members during the viewing or conversation. During the Preparatory Session, your group will discuss how to respond to various emotions should they surface during the study. To get ready for that discussion, you will be guided in thinking through how others have responded to your emotions in the past.

DAY 1

Morning: Today's stride is to consider how your emotions were responded to in your family of origin. Look at the Feelings Chart on page 16. When you expressed a certain feeling, what kind of reception did it get? For example, how OK was it for you to be happy—and not just to be happy, but to express that happiness in different ways such as smiling, laughing, playing, or dancing? Was it always OK or was it OK only sometimes? For instance, was it only OK to be happy when mom was happy or when your grades were up? Or, when it comes to anger, was it OK for you to feel and express anger, or was anger only OK for your dad? Or, if you were sad and cried, were your tears condoned, or were you sent to your room until you could "dry up"?

For each feeling, and each behavior associated with the feeling, jot an FO for "family of origin" in appropriate box. For greater effect, utilize a pack of multicolor pens, crayons, or markers. For today's exercise, choose a particular color to represent your family of origin. (Over the next week, you will also consider how other groups of people have responded to your emotions, so leave room on the chart to add more initials.)

As an example, let's say that when you were happy in your family of origin, it was mostly OK to smile and laugh, it was sometimes OK to play, and it was never OK to dance, your chart would look like this:

	Never OK	Sometimes OK	Mostly OK	Always OK
Happy			FO	
Smiling			FO	
Laughing			FO	
Playing		FO		
Dancing	FO			

If your mom and dad responded very differently to your emotions, you may prefer to choose a separate color or initials representing mom, dad, or stepparents.

Go with your first impression. If you get stuck, simply imagine yourself as a child standing in front of your parents displaying that emotion and notice what happens next in your imagination.

After completing the exercise, what are you led to say to God?

Evening: Look back at the Feelings Chart. Were some emotions OK for others in your family to exhibit but not for you? Which emotions were OK for whom?

_____
_____
_____
_____
_____

What was done to curtail or prohibit certain feelings?

_____
_____
_____
_____
_____
_____
_____
_____

What was done to condone or encourage other feelings?

_____

_____

_____

_____

_____

_____

_____

_____

Before going to sleep, try to express your current emotions, whatever they are, to your Father in heaven.

_____

_____

_____

_____

_____

_____

_____

_____

_____

_____

_____

_____

_____

_____

_____

_____

_____

_____

_____

_____

FEELINGS CHART

	Never OK	Sometimes OK	Mostly OK	Always OK
HAPPY				
Smiling				
Laughing				
Playing				
Dancing				
CONFIDENT				
Dreaming				
Asserting				
Daring				
Succeeding				
PEACEFUL				
Nurturing				
Loving				
Resting				
Waiting				
SAD				
Withdrawing				
Moping				
Crying				
Quitting				
ANGRY				
Scowling				
Complaining				
Yelling				
Doubting				
FEARFUL				
Fretting				
Clinging				
Wavering				
Running				

DAY 2

Morning: Consider the Feelings Chart again. How were emotions and their corresponding behaviors responded to in the church or faith community in which you grew up? Which were OK and which were not? Choose a color for church or use the letter C and mark your answers on the chart. If you attended multiple churches, either generalize the responses or choose the church that had the most influence on you. If you didn't grow up attending a church, choose another important institution to consider, possibly your school, sports league, or scout troop.

After completing the exercise, what do you find yourself saying to God?

Evening: What effect did your childhood faith community have on how you relate to emotions?

_____
_____
_____
_____
_____
_____

List the emotions you are aware of feeling right now.

_____
_____
_____
_____
_____
_____

Try to simply tell Jesus these emotions: "Jesus, I am feeling…"

_____
_____
_____
_____
_____
_____

How did you feel as you told Jesus your current emotions? Was it easy or difficult, comfortable or awkward?

_____

_____

_____

_____

_____

DAY 3

Morning: How does your current family respond to various feelings? Choose a color to represent your current family or jot CF in the suitable spaces on the Feelings Chart.

After doing so, tell God your reaction.

Evening: Look at the primary emotions highlighted in bold on the chart (see list, below). What happens in your current family when each of these is expressed? What verbal or behavioral reaction are they likely to get? Will they be joined ("I feel that, too"), minimized ("It's not that bad"; "That's nothing to get excited about"), pushed away ("Come back when you aren't like this"), or ignored altogether? Try to be specific.

Happy: _____

_____

_____

Confident: _____

_____

_____

Peaceful: _____

_____

_____

Sad: _____

_____

_____

Angry: _____

_____

_____

Fearful: _____

_____

_____

Think of an emotion someone expressed in your family today and note how you responded to it.

_____

_____

_____

_____

_____

Close by praying for that person.

DAY 4

Morning: What is your internal reaction when you feel each emotion? Do you tend to welcome the emotion and try to learn from it, or are you more likely to ignore or suppress the emotion? Choose a color to represent you, or mark your initials on the Feelings Chart corresponding with how OK you are with each emotion and its related behaviors.

Be especially aware of your emotions today.

Evening: Choose one emotion you are not comfortable expressing, and try expressing it to Jesus.

Write below what it was like expressing this emotion to Jesus.

_____

_____

_____

_____

_____

DAY 5

Morning: In your small group gatherings, how do you sense emotions and their related behaviors are received? Choose a color to denote your small group or mark with SG on the Feelings Chart.

Evening: For each primary emotion below, write what reaction you would want to receive if you displayed it in your small group. Also note the reaction you think you would receive if you showed that emotion.

	Reaction I would want	Reaction I would receive
Happy	_____	_____
Confident	_____	_____
Peaceful	_____	_____
Sad	_____	_____
Angry	_____	_____
Fearful	_____	_____

On the Feelings Chart, put a check mark beside the emotions and behaviors that you would feel comfortable exhibiting in your small group.

What will you pray for your small group concerning emotions?

_____
_____
_____
_____
_____

DAY 6

Morning: What is your sense of God's reaction to your various emotions and their associated behaviors? Which is he OK with all the time, mostly, sometimes, and never? Choose a color for God or mark with a G.

As you experience emotions today, notice whether you are thinking God approves or disapproves.

Evening: When Jesus walked the earth, which emotions do you think he experienced and accepted? Mark with a chosen color or with JC on the Feelings Chart.

Look over the chart with its colors or initials. What do you observe?

_____
_____
_____
_____
_____
_____
_____
_____
_____
_____
_____
_____

What will you pray for yourself regarding emotions?

_____
_____
_____
_____
_____
_____
_____
_____
_____
_____
_____
_____

PREPARATORY SESSION: NOTES
(to be completed with your small group)

Matthew 20:34 _____

26:37– 38 _____

Mark 3:5 _____

7:34 _____

8:12 _____

10:13–14 _____

10:21 _____

Luke 7:9 _____

7:12–13 _____

10:21 _____

12:50 _____

19:41 _____

22:15 _____

John 2:14–17 _____

11:31–35, 38 _____

12:27; 13:21 _____

GROUP AGREEMENT

In our group, we will...

___ welcome the sharing of struggles and deep emotions

___ limit the sharing or struggles and deep emotions, and encourage those who wish to work through deep emotions to seek out a supplemental setting in which to do so, such as a support group or counseling situation

When a person in our group expresses happy, confident, or peaceful emotions, we will ...

and we will not...

When a person expresses sad, angry, or fearful emotions, we will ...

and we will not...

ACTS OF GOD

PREPARATORY SESSION

Daily Strides AFTER the Preparatory Session

The Daily Strides in this section are designed to follow the Preparatory Session and prepare the group for either viewing the Acts of God feature film or, if your group is not going to view the feature film, viewing Episode 1 of the Acts of God study.

This week you will consider the degree to which you are OK with others having and expressing their emotions.

Days 1–5: Morning

1. Each day, choose a different category from the list below:

spouse

best friend

children

grandchildren

parents

spiritual leaders

students or those you shepherd spiritually

God/Jesus

2. Think of someone specific from that category
   (There is space designated to write their name on the following pages).

3. Choose a color or symbol for that person.

4. Mark the suitable squares on the Feelings Chart on page 29.

Example: On Day 1, you might choose "grandchildren" (that sounds relatively easy!). Next, choose one of your grandchildren. Let's say her name is Sophie. Then work through the Feelings Chart, asking yourself, How OK am I that Sophie is happy and that she expresses her happiness through smiling, laughing, playing, or dancing? Is that always OK, mostly OK, sometimes OK, or never OK? After you mark the appropriate box with her color, continue through all the emotions in the same way.

After filling in the chart each morning, notice what are you led to pray for the person you chose, take that prayer to the Father.

Days 1–5: Evening

Each evening, note which emotion you scored as most difficult for you to accept in this person, and then try this helpful exercise:

1. Imagine the person feeling and expressing this difficult emotion. Get a clear picture in your mind.

2. Once you have a clear picture, imagine Jesus in the scene, coming to the person. Envision how he or she expresses that emotion to Jesus.

3. Based on your knowledge of the Gospels and the direction of the Spirit, how do you believe Jesus would react to this person and the strong emotions? In your mind's eye, see Jesus responding in this very way.

4. Now imagine yourself stepping into this scene. As you enter the picture, see Jesus turning to you and asking to enter you, to come into your mind and heart. Agree to have him enter. See him step into you and become one with you.

5. Now that Jesus is in you, allow him to work through you, to do for this person what he was doing before, only now through you.

6. Notice what this is like for you and the other person.

7. Complete the exercise by praying for this person.

Write your reaction to this exercise each day:

DAY 1: Person chosen: _____

Emotion most difficult to be OK with: _____

Reaction to imagination exercise: _____

_____

_____

_____

DAY 2: Person chosen: _____

Emotion most difficult to be OK with: _____

Reaction to imagination exercise: _____

_____

_____

_____

DAY 3: Person chosen: _____

Emotion most difficult to be OK with: _____

Reaction to imagination exercise: _____

_____

_____

DAY 4: Person chosen: _____

Emotion most difficult to be OK with: _____

Reaction to imagination exercise: _____

_____

_____

_____

DAY 5: Person chosen: _____

Emotion most difficult to be OK with: _____

Reaction to imagination exercise: _____

_____

_____

_____

DAY 6

Morning: Pick one person out of those you chose this week. Contact this person sometime today in person, by phone, or via email. Explain that you are working on an exercise regarding how you deal with others' emotions. Ask if he or she would be willing to discuss how you respond to his or her emotions.

Let's say the person you chose is your best friend, Debbie. If Debbie is willing, ask her how she perceives your responses to her various emotions. Do this by going down the Feelings Chart, asking how she perceives you responding to her happiness, smiling, laughing, and so on. For each feeling, also ask her what kind of response she wishes from you.

When you have gone through the whole chart, thank this person for his or her willingness to help you grow as a person.

Evening: Write your reactions to the conversation in the space below.

_____
_____
_____
_____
_____
_____
_____
_____

How do you find yourself praying for yourself – and this person – in light of this discussion?

_____
_____
_____
_____
_____
_____
_____
_____

FEELINGS CHART

	Never OK	Sometimes OK	Mostly OK	Always OK
HAPPY				
Smiling				
Laughing				
Playing				
Dancing				
CONFIDENT				
Dreaming				
Asserting				
Daring				
Succeeding				
PEACEFUL				
Nurturing				
Loving				
Resting				
Waiting				
SAD				
Withdrawing				
Moping				
Crying				
Quitting				
ANGRY				
Scowling				
Complaining				
Yelling				
Doubting				
FEARFUL				
Fretting				
Clinging				
Wavering				
Running				

ACTS OF GOD

SIX LIVES.
ONE QUESTION.
WHY?

ACTS OF GOD

AFTER VIEWING THE MOVIE

DAILY STRIDES AFTER VIEWING THE MOVIE

The Daily Strides in this section are designed to follow the group viewing of the Acts of God feature film. If your group viewed the film, walk through these steps.

DAY 1

Morning: It's natural when viewing a feature film to evaluate the production quality, plot structure, acting skills, and other such elements. So let's get those thoughts out of the way. Jot down any evaluative reactions to the Acts of God film: what you did and didn't like, what you wish had been different, what you thought was good, what you found unrealistic, and so forth.

_____

_____

_____

_____

What emotions did you feel while watching the feature film, and what did you find yourself doing with those emotions? Fill out the Feelings Chart on page 32.

- If you didn't feel a particular emotion, check the first column.

- If you did feel the emotion, and found yourself allowing the emotion but not deeply connecting with it, mark the second column.

- If you felt the emotion, and found yourself fully entering and embracing the emotion, check the third column.

- If you felt the emotion but found yourself resisting, denying, or suppressing it, check the last column.

After completing the Feelings Chart, look back over **the emotions you fully embraced**. See if one emotion stands out in some way. If none do, simply choose one emotion.

Write that emotion on the palm of your hand with an ink pen. As you go through your day, whenever you notice the word on your palm, invite the Holy Spirit to teach you about that emotion. This teaching may involve validating this emotion as a gift from God, helping you locate this emotion inside you, showing you how to better employ this emotion, or guiding you in discerning this emotion in others.

FEELINGS CHART

	Didn't Feel	Felt & Allowed	Felt & Embraced	Felt & Resisted
HAPPY				
Pleased				
Excited				
Playful				
Sensuous				
CONFIDENT				
Powerful				
Daring				
Worthwhile				
Successful				
PEACEFUL				
Grateful				
Loving				
Nurturing				
Relaxed				
SAD			✓	
Lonely				
Heartbroken			✗	
Guilty				
Bored				
ANGRY		✓		
Annoyed				
Critical				
Hurt				
Skeptical				
FEARFUL				
Anxious		✓		
Needy				
Uncertain				
Inadequate				

Evening: Record your experience with the emotion you chose this morning.

_____

_____

_____

_____

_____

_____

_____

_____

Turn to your Preparatory Session notes from the Small Group time on page 22. From the list of emotions Jesus is described as having, find one similar to the emotion you chose to consider today. Look up the passage and read the surrounding story.

Do you find yourself believing that Jesus experienced this emotion as fully and deeply as you do? If so, what is it like for you recognizing this affinity? If not, try to describe why it is hard for you to see Jesus feeling in such a human way.

_____

_____

_____

_____

_____

_____

_____

_____

How are you led to pray?

_____

_____

_____

_____

_____

_____

_____

DAY 2

Morning: Look over yesterday's Feelings Chart. Notice **the emotions you resisted, denied or suppressed**. As you do, see if one emotion stands out in some way. If none do, simply choose one emotion.

Write that emotion on the palm of your other hand with an ink pen. Whenever you notice that word as you go through your day, invite the Holy Spirit to teach you about that emotion. This teaching may involve validating this emotion as a gift from God, helping you locate this emotion inside you, showing you how to better employ this emotion, or guiding you in discerning this emotion in others.

Evening: Record your experience with the emotion you chose this morning.

_____
_____
_____
_____
_____
_____
_____

How was your experience of the emotion you chose for today different from that of the emotion focused on yesterday?

_____
_____
_____
_____
_____
_____
_____

Turn to your Preparatory Session notes on page 22 again. From the list of emotions Jesus is described as having, find one similar to the emotion you chose to consider today. Look up the passage and read the surrounding story.

Do you find yourself believing that Jesus experienced this emotion as fully and deeply as you do? If so, what is like for you recognizing this affinity? If not, try to describe why it is hard for you to see Jesus feeling in such a human way.

_____

_____

_____

_____

_____

_____

_____

What are you led to pray?

_____

_____

_____

_____

_____

_____

DAY 3

Morning: As you watched the film, did you find yourself identifying with any particular character? If so, describe the reasons for this sense of connection.

_____

_____

_____

_____

_____

_____

_____

As you go through your day, notice if you connect in a similar way with anyone you happen to encounter.

Evening: Think about the character in the film with whom you most identified. Can you think of a biblical character who is similar in some way? Write the biblical character's name on the space below:

_____

Meditate on this biblical person. You may want to find and read some of the person's story in your Bible. As you do, what reactions do you have? Are you comforted? Challenged? Instructed in some way? Record your thoughts below.

_____
_____
_____
_____
_____
_____
_____

DAY 4

Morning: What do you consider to be the worst things that can happen in life, the things that most challenge the idea that there is a good God who really cares?

_____
_____
_____
_____
_____
_____
_____

How do you find yourself praying when you hear of such things occurring?

_____
_____
_____
_____
_____
_____
_____

What do you pray as you face this day?

_____

_____

_____

_____

_____

_____

_____

Evening: How have you reconciled (or tried to reconcile) the concept of a good God with the ever-present level of suffering in this world?

_____

_____

_____

_____

_____

_____

_____

_____

In his letter, Jesus' half-brother James advised those who lacked wisdom to ask God for it. The context for his advice was not career, money, or marriage but had to do with suffering and how to respond. Ask for wisdom regarding the meaning of suffering. You may want to read the section of Scripture in James 1:1–12.

As you pray and read, what insights come to mind?

_____

_____

_____

_____

_____

_____

_____

DAY 5

Morning: List your closest friends and family members down the left column of the chart below. In the middle column, note the hard things each person has faced in the past. In the right column, add the difficult issues they are facing currently.

Name	Past difficulties / sufferings	Current difficulties / sufferings

What is your immediate reaction to this list?

_____

_____

_____

_____

_____

_____

How are you led to pray?

As you completed the exercise, did any one name stand out? If not, choose one of the names now. Consider how you might cheer on this person today —through a note, a small gift, a phone call, or in some other way.

Evening: As you thought about the person you chose today, and the struggles he or she has experienced, what was the effect on you?

_____

_____

_____

_____

_____

_____

_____

Did you find your feelings about this person, or sense of connection to this person, affected in any way? If so, how?

_____

_____

_____

_____

_____

_____

_____

Look back at emotions attributed to Jesus from your Preparatory Session Notes on page 22. Which emotion from the list do you feel when you think of your chosen person? Look up that passage and read the surrounding story.

In prayer, imagine this person fully receiving this emotion first from Jesus, then from you. For example, if you chose "compassion," then visualize your chosen person meeting Jesus, seeing his compassion, and fully accepting it; then meeting you, seeing your compassion, and fully receiving your concern.

DAY 6

Morning: List the members of your study group in the left column. If you can't recall or don't know all of their names, list the names of those you do. In the middle column, note the hard things each person has faced in the past. In the right column, add the difficult issues they are facing currently.

Name	Past difficulties / sufferings	Current difficulties / sufferings

What is your immediate reaction to this list?

How are you led to pray?

As you completed the exercise, did any one name stand out? If so, consider how you might cheer on this person today—through a note, a small gift, a phone call, or in some other way.

Evening: As you thought about the person you chose today, and the struggles he or she has experienced, what was the effect on you?

_____

_____

_____

_____

_____

_____

_____

Did you find your feelings about this person, or sense of connection to this person, affected in any way? If so, how?

_____

_____

_____

_____

_____

_____

_____

Look back at emotions attributed to Jesus from your Preparatory Session Notes on page 22. Which emotion from the list do you feel when you think of your chosen person? Look up that passage and read the surrounding story.

In prayer, imagine this person fully receiving this emotion first from Jesus, then from you.

ACTS OF GOD

PROBLEM WITH PAIN

EPISODE 1: THE PROBLEM OF PAIN

Notes from Small Group session:

_____
_____
_____
_____
_____
_____
_____
_____
_____
_____
_____
_____
_____
_____
_____
_____
_____
_____
_____
_____
_____

Possible reactions to suffering:

become bitter   withdraw

feel defeated   turn to alcohol or drugs

become defiant   contemplate suicide

trust God   _____

_____   _____

_____   _____

_____   _____

The problem of suffering has always been a major challenge to belief in God. If God is all-powerful and all-loving, why does he allow horrible things to happen to such good people? Cynics conclude either God doesn't care or he is incapable of intervening.

Leslie Weatherhead once suggested that there are three areas to God's will: God's intended will, his permissive will, and his ultimate will. God intended this world to be perfect when he created it, but he permitted men to have freedom of choice, and as a result sin entered into the world. The sin virus knocked the world off-kilter. God has temporarily permitted pain and tragedy as a result.

We are not puppets on a string. We are free human beings created in the image of God and given the privilege of moving about in an eciting but fallen and sometimes dangerous world. Occasionally we're going to crash and draw blood, but the heavenly Father promises, "I'll be there. I'll go through it with you, and if you let me, I'll see to it that even the most painful eperience will mature you, help you appreciate what Jesus went through, and make you hungry for heaven where I'm going to wipe away all tears, and there will be no more pain or sorrow and I will make all things right."

DAILY STRIDES FOLLOWING EPISODE 1

This week's Daily Strides focus primarily on the intellectual problem of evil and suffering. However, we're going to avoid looking at the issue in a detached, theoretical way. We're not going to ask general questions like: Why is there suffering in the world? Why do bad things happen to those people over there? Or how can other people deal with their calamities? Rather, we are going to ask: What do I discover about the suffering that directly affects me? And what is my experience with suffering showing me?

The reason we are framing the question of God and suffering in this personal way is that, in reality, we can only know our own story. We can't really know the stories of others. As a case in point, you might be acquainted with someone who is facing a situation you consider intolerable: a debilitating injury or a chronic-pain disorder. Yet that person tells you, "This difficult situation is the best thing that has ever happened to me. I have more peace now than ever before." What she says sounds unbelievable, but that's because you can't know what is going on inside other people, what insights they have gained, or what help they have received.

Or maybe you have ventured out on a mission trip to an impoverished country only to find that many of the nationals living in squalor appear happier and more content than your healthy, wealthy, air-conditioned neighbors. How can this be? I can't imagine having their spirit under these circumstances. Right, because their story is not your story.

On the other hand, perhaps you know someone who has experienced what appeared to be a minor setback such as a job loss or temporary financial blow only to hear later that he collapsed into depression or even took his own life. You wonder how something that appeared so minor could lead to such a tragic reaction.

Others' stories are always hidden to us. We cannot really get into the head or heart of the African orphan, the aging invalid, or even the wealthy celebrity. We can only truly know our own story and even that in a limited way. So your Daily Strides will focus on your story. This week you will look at how you experience your freewill in relation to suffering.

DAY 1

Morning: We begin with an uncomfortable question: What suffering have you caused others? Who have you hurt? What have you done that caused pain to your parents, siblings, friends, spouse, children, or church members? You may not have accidently taken a little girl's life while driving drunk, but be honest about what evil you have done to others. Did you scar a sibling with your childhood teasing, break the heart of your parents with your drinking, steal the virginity of a naïve date, crush the spirit of your children with your criticism, kill the joy of your spouse with pornography, disillusion fellow believers with your hypocrisy?

The idea here is not to beat ourselves up with all the bad things we've done but to look into one aspect of the reality of evil by more clearly seeing our own evil. Begin your list now on the next page. Ask the Holy Spirt to guide you. Then continue to think about the question during your day.

_____

_____

_____

_____

_____

_____

_____

_____

_____

_____

_____

_____

_____

_____

_____

_____

_____

_____

Evening: Add anything to your list that came to mind during the day. Write your reactions to this list.

_____

_____

_____

_____

What do you find yourself saying to Jesus about your list?

_____

_____

_____

_____

How do you want Jesus to respond to the ways you have hurt others?

_____

_____

_____

_____

DAY 2

Morning: Look over your list from yesterday. Which offense do you consider the worst or to have the worst consequences on others? Choose one and circle it.

Next, ask yourself, Should God have stopped me from doing this? Again, keep the answer personal. The question is not whether God should have stopped Hitler or the rapist across town or even your dad from hurting you. The question today is: Should God have stopped me from doing this bad thing (or series of things) I did? Journal your response.

_____
_____
_____
_____
_____
_____
_____
_____
_____
_____
_____
_____
_____
_____
_____
_____
_____
_____
_____
_____
_____
_____
_____

Continue to think about this question during your day. As you are tempted to do something low, selfish, or harmful, ask yourself: Should God directly stop me from doing what I am attracted to doing?

Evening: During your morning exercise, you asked yourself, should God have stopped me from doing this bad thing?

1) If you answered yes, God should have stopped me, describe how you think God should have done it. Avoid the response that says God is God so he should be able to find some way to stop me without violating my freedom to choose. That's a non-answer, a cop-out, a form of magical thinking. Some things are intrinsically impossible; that is, they carry their impossibility within them. C. S. Lewis put it this way:

You may attribute miracles to [God], but not nonsense. This is no limit to His power. If you choose to say, "God can give a creature free will and at the same time withhold free will from it," you have not succeeded in saying anything about God: meaningless combinations of words do not suddenly acquire meaning simply because we prefix to them the two other words, "God can." It remains true that all things are possible with God: the intrinsic impossibilities are not things but nonentities. It is no more possible for God than for the weakest of His creatures to carry out both of two mutually exclusive alternatives; not because His power meets an obstacle, but because nonsense remains nonsense even when we talk it about God (The Problem of Pain, [London: Fontana Books, 1957], 16).

So, practically speaking, how should God have stopped you from doing the hurtful thing you did? Should he have struck you dead? Paralyzed your limbs? Made you sick? Erased the bad thoughts from your brain? Appeared to you in a vision and talked you out of it? Instantaneously healed your soul so you wouldn't desire this evil thing at all? Prompted someone to catch you doing it early on, before the consequences got too bad? Try to put your answer into words.

_____

_____

_____

_____

_____

_____

2) If this morning you answered no, God should not have stopped me, explain why you think he shouldn't have in spite of the pain your actions caused yourself and others.

_____

_____

_____

_____

_____

_____

_____

Now ask God why he didn't stop you. Take time to consider what the Holy Spirit may be saying here.

Review the life of Jesus in your mind, or flip through the Gospels, and see if you can identify an occasion when Jesus decisively stopped someone from doing evil, when he acted in a way in which another person could not resist his will but had to do what Jesus commanded. Write below what you come up with.

_____

_____

_____

_____

_____

_____

_____

DAY 3

Morning: Our stride today is to think about the natural consequences of yesterday's responses.

1) If God had completely stopped you from doing this bad thing so that there was no possible way you could have followed through with the evil deed, what would be the consequences of him stopping you?

- Would you have become (   ) more free or (   ) less free as a person? Explain.

  _____

  _____

  _____

  _____

  _____

- Would you have developed (   ) more character or (   ) less character? Explain.

  _____

  _____

  _____

  _____

  _____

- Would you have developed (   ) more respect for God or (   ) less? Explain.

  _____

  _____

  _____

  _____

  _____

- Would you then have wanted God to control (   ) more of your actions in the same way or (   ) not control more of your actions in the same way? Explain.

  _____

  _____

  _____

  _____

  _____

- Would you come to (   ) love God more or (   ) less? Explain.

  _____

  _____

  _____

  _____

  _____

2) If you said God shouldn't have stopped you, what were the consequences of him not doing so? These consequences are less hypothetical because there were observable, concrete consequences to your actions. Name as many consequences as you can think of, for both you and others.

_____
_____
_____
_____
_____
_____
_____
_____
_____
_____
_____
_____
_____
_____

Evening: We often wish God would stop evil "out there" but may not like it when God interferes with our freedom of choice. We can behave like a child who screams, "Mom! Make my brother share his toys!" but resents it when mom makes her share her toys. We want God to control others but resent it when we feel God is controlling us. When God doesn't control others, we say he is uncaring, monstrous, or doesn't exist at all. When we feel God is controlling us, we say he is intrusive, pushy, or domineering.

What is your reaction to the previous paragraph?

_____
_____
_____
_____
_____
_____

How will you pray concerning God and his degree of control over you?

DAY 4

Morning: So far this week you have looked at how much you think God should control your actions. Now let's expand the issue from just your actions to your overall character. Garrett Connors, the man in the movie who collided into Sarah's car, appears to be arrogant, self-centered, manipulative, and condescending. While driving drunk is what Connors did, arrogant is what he is; arrogance is part of his character, his developed being.

Today, look at yourself. How would you describe your character at this point in your life? Loving? Generous? Fearful? Ambitious? Pushy? Happy-go-lucky? Attempt a description.

_____
_____
_____
_____
_____
_____
_____
_____
_____
_____
_____
_____
_____
_____

Ask the Holy Spirit for any further insights into your character. How would he describe you? Write what comes to mind below.

_____
_____
_____
_____
_____
_____
_____

During the day, pay attention to your developed character to see what else you might observe.

Evening: What else did you notice about your character today?

_____

_____

_____

_____

_____

_____

_____

_____

_____

If Garrett Connors were a real person rather than a movie figure, we might wonder how he came to have this particular character. We might ask if the way he turned out was all his doing. Or was he spoiled as a child? What if he had been told over and over that he was superior and others were here to serve him? Or what if he had been wounded by a busy, disinterested dad or an abusive, narcissistic mom? What if no one has ever really loved him? Or what if a competitive bent runs deep in his DNA? Is Connors' personality all his doing, or is some of the responsibility to be shared?

When considering questions like these, a helpful concept is "percentage of responsibility." Is Garrett Connors 100 percent responsible for his character, or do nature and nurture have some part to play? Again, we don't know another person's story. We can't know why they are as they are. But we do know our own story, at least in part.

Think about two aspects of your character, one you consider good and one you consider not so good. Try to name the factors that have led to having each of these character traits. For example, if you have a tender heart, you might say part of the reason is your mom's genes; she's tender, too. Or maybe one factor has to do with all the losses you've suffered. Or maybe you have intentionally worked hard to empathize with others. Try to list the factors in the good aspect of your character. Then do the same with a negative aspect of your character.

Positive aspect of my character: _____

Reasons I'm like this:

- _____
- _____
- _____
- _____
- _____
- _____
- _____
- _____
- _____
- _____

Negative aspect of my character: _____

Reasons I'm like this:

- _____
- _____
- _____
- _____
- _____
- _____
- _____
- _____
- _____
- _____

Did you include cultural forces like TV, music, or schooling? How about other relational influences such as grandparents, teachers, coaches, and ministers? Would you say spiritual forces like God or Satan have been involved? If so, add these to your list above.

Give each of the factors you listed a percentage according to how much responsibility you think that factor has had in making you the way you are. Jot the number beside the factor.

For example, Elizabeth may believe that "tenderness genes" inherited from her mom account for 25 percent of her tender heart, so she would write 25% beside "mom's genes." The hard events in Elizabeth's life might account for 10 percent, while her own efforts to become empathetic account for 20 percent, and so forth.

Next add up all the percentages you just listed.
What's the total for each? Positive _____% Negative _____%

If your total is more than 100 percent, something is out of balance (since percentage means a proportion stated in hundredths). If you have more than 100 percent in your total, think about what needs to be revised so the total adds up to 100 percent.

Adjust your percentages to add up to 100 percent. You may resist doing so, saying, "I am 100 percent responsible for my choices and therefore for my character." But is that the true reality of your life? If you hadn't been born with the "tenderness genes," would you really be so tender? If you had never had anything bad happen to you, would you be so empathetic? If God wasn't at work in your spirit, could you have grown as you have? See if you can adjust your percentages to total 100 percent.

One reason for doing this exercise is to highlight how complex causation is, how many factors come into play in just one facet of life.

What will you pray concerning these two aspects of your character?

_____
_____
_____
_____
_____
_____
_____
_____

DAYS 5

Morning: As you worked on the percentage-of-responsibility exercise, did you find yourself wishing the world were more simple, clear-cut, and uncomplicated? Or did you find yourself intrigued by the extreme complexity and interrelatedness of the world?

As you go through your day, be aware of your reactions to what happens.
☐ Do you tend to find simple reasons for occurrences? "She's just mean, that's all there is to it." "Satan gave him cancer." "It was God's will; that's why I got promoted."

☐ Do you tend to resist simple answers and embrace the unfathomable complexity? "I'm not sure why she acted that way; we're complicated people." "I can't be certain why he has cancer as there are many possible causes." "I think there are several factors for me being promoted, but I'm grateful to God for his part in it."

Evening: Think about the typical teaching you have heard in church. In your experience, has the teaching tended to acknowledge the incredible complexity of life or has it tended toward the simplistic? Jot down your thoughts.

_____

_____

_____

_____

_____

_____

_____

_____

Would you say the Scriptures lend themselves to a simple or complex explanation for things? Again, jot down your thoughts.

_____

_____

_____

_____

_____

_____

_____

_____

Pray in whatever way you feel led to close out your day.

DAY 6

Morning: Read the passages that will be highlighted in the next episode, Genesis 37 and 39:1–6. As you do, write down who says and does what.

Who   What they say and/or do

_____   _____

_____   _____

_____   _____

_____   _____

_____   _____

What do you see in this part of Joseph's story that God definitely caused to happen?

_____

_____

_____

_____

_____

_____

As you experience your day, ask yourself periodically: What do I see happening around me that I can definitely say God caused to happen?

Evening: What did you see today that you feel certain God made happen?

_____

_____

_____

_____

_____

_____

_____

_____

_____

_____

_____

_____

What did you cause to happen today? Make a quick list.

_____
_____
_____
_____
_____
_____
_____
_____
_____
_____

What part, if any, do you perceive God played in what you caused to happen?

_____
_____
_____
_____
_____
_____
_____
_____
_____
_____

How do you find yourself praying in light of today's exercise?

_____
_____
_____
_____
_____
_____
_____
_____
_____
_____

NOTES:

FAITHFUL DESPITE BETRAYAL

EPISODE 2: FAITHFUL DESPITE BETRAYAL

Notes from Small Group session:

_____

_____

_____

_____

_____

_____

_____

_____

_____

_____

_____

Sarah's feeling	Sarah's thought
_____	_____
_____	_____
_____	_____
_____	_____

"When our Chihuahua, Chili Pepper, died, I said, 'Harold, the Lord picks out certain people for suffering, and the good book said that we're supposed to rejoice when that happens.' I know just how you feel, but that's what you've got to do sweetie, rejoice."

"You know, we all have our crosses to bear. Honey, you just tell me if there's anything I can do to help. I know this world's hard. It's just a vale of tears. First, your husband, then your little girl. You're still young. You still got a heap of heartache coming. But God never gives us more than we can handle."

Other unhelpful statements:
  Get over it. Just say no.

_____

_____

_____

_____

_____

_____

DAILY STRIDES

DAY 1

Morning or Evening: If your group ended their gathering with a meditative prayer (which was optional for the leader), then write your thoughts and feelings regarding that experience.

_____

_____

_____

_____

_____

_____

_____

_____

_____

_____

_____

_____

_____

If your group did not go through the prayer exercise, read through the following, and decide if it is something you'd like to do on your own. If your group did do the exercise, read through it again, noting what was particulary meaningful to you.

We'll close our time with a period of quiet reflection where you'll be encouraged to meet with Jesus and invite him into your grief. The basis for this reflection is that while thoughts are eperienced in our heads, emotions are eperienced in our bodies. For eample, when we are worried, the concerns will be running through our brains, but the anious feelings will be found in our bodies, eperienced as tightness in the shoulders or butterflies in the stomach.

This realization eplains why talking about suffering and reading verses of comfort may not actually bring emotional healing. Our minds may have better understanding but our feelings are unaf - fected. The commonplace remark, "I know it in my head, I just don't feel it in my heart," points to this reality.

The purpose of this reflection is to help us become aware of how and where we tend to experience and store our sadness, and then invite Jesus to meet us there. We realize that quiet reflection is not a common practice in a typical study, but this isn't a typical study. We are dealing with the most gut-wrenching and heart-breaking (and notice the bodily terms, GUT-wrenching; HEART-breaking) issues of life. So we want to find not just intellectual understanding but also emotional healing. We encourage you to give yourself fully to this reflection and see what God might do through it. This reflection will last about ten minutes.

Take a comfortable posture, suitable to you for quiet reflection.

Let's begin by just taking in the words of David in Psalms 139:

You have searched me, Lord, and you know me.
You know when I sit and when I rise;
    you perceive my thoughts from afar.
You discern my going out and my lying down;
    you are familiar with all my ways.
Before a word is on my tongue
    you, Lord, know it completely.
You hem me in behind and before,
    and you lay your hand upon me.
Such knowledge is too wonderful for me,
    too lofty for me to attain.
Where can I go from your Spirit?
    Where can I flee from your presence?
If I go up to the heavens, you are there;
    if I make my bed in the depths, you are there.
If I rise on the wings of the dawn,
    if I settle on the far side of the sea,
even there your hand will guide me,
    your right hand will hold me fast.
If I say, "Surely the darkness will hide me
    and the light become night around me,"
even the darkness will not be dark to you;
    the night will shine like the day,
    for darkness is as light to you.

For you created my inmost being;
  you knit me together in my mother's womb. …
Search me, God, and know my heart;
  test me and know my anxious thoughts.
See if there is any offensive way in me,
  and lead me in the way everlasting **(Psalm 139:1–24).**

Allow the Holy Spirit to search you—in order to find any grief within you. Where have you stored your sadness, your pain? Grief that isn't worked out gets stored up, and its storehouse is in the body. Where have you stored your sorrow? Is it in your shoulders, living there as tightness and tension? (Short pause.) Is your grief in your chest, the feeling of heartache or heartbreak? (Short pause.) Or is your grief in your gut, a pit in your stomach or a weight in your lower abdomen? (Short pause.) Allow the Spirit to search you, to show you your anxious grief, to open your awareness to where you store your sorrow. (Longer pause.)

Feel or sense this pocket of pain, this area of sadness. Notice how it feels. How big is this area? Is it large? Is it small? What do you sense? (Short pause.) How heavy or weighty is this area of sorrow? Is it a few ounces? A few pounds? (Short pause.)

In Isaiah, Jesus is called "a man of sorrows, acquainted with deepest grief" (Isaiah 53:3, New Living Translation). In Hebrews we are told Jesus can sympathize with our weaknesses because he was made like us in every way (Hebrews 2:17; 4:15). The word sympathize simply means to "feel with." Since Jesus is acquainted with sorrow and pain, he can feel our sorrow with us. He not only can feel our heartache, he wants to feel our heart-ache. He wants to be the friend who sticks closer than a brother (Proverbs 18:24). So invite him close to you now. Invite him to come alongside. By faith, sense his presence. See his eyes of compassion, if you can. Allow him to sit beside you, to feel with you. Allow him to touch this place in your body where the grief is stored. Or you might even allow him to enter this place in you and sit with you in your grief. (Pause.)

In John's Gospel, the story is told of Jesus coming to the tomb of his friend Lazarus. There he saw Mary weeping. It says he was deeply moved and troubled in his spirit, and he too wept (John 11:33, 35.) Can you allow Jesus to come to the tomb of your grief, and simply sit with you, to be where you are without rebuke or judgment, to simply sympathize with you, to feel what you feel, and to be fully with you in the deepest aspect of your pain? Can you share your sorrow with him? (Longer pause.)

Hear Jesus say, "I am with you. I am here with you. I will never leave you nor forsake you. Never. I will not leave you as an orphan in your grief. I will be with you always, even to the end of the age" (Hebrews 13:5; John 14:18; Matthew 28:20). Allow yourself to experience his presence, his simple presence in the center of your sadness. (Longer pause.)

Now anchor this sense of Christ's compassionate presence with you. Jesus is with you in your pain; he is indeed Immanuel, God with us, God with you. Say to yourself, Christ is with me; Jesus is with me in my pain. This is faith, to believe and experience what is promised, to embrace this reality, to hold fast to his promised presence. Accept his comfort. Rest in his soothing, loving presence. (Longer pause.)

Take this sense of Jesus' nearness, his understanding, his comfort with you. Even as you slowly re-engage the world, be filled with Christ. Amen.

DAY 2

Morning: The shortest, and one of the most comforting, verse in the Bible simple reads "Jesus wept." Read the story that contains that verse in John 11:1-44. As you do, notice Jesus' confidence in verses 4, 11, and 25-26.

Considering that confidence, why do you think Jesus was so deeply moved to the point of tears in verses 33, 35, and 38?

How are the two aspects of this story reconciled, Jesus being so confident of resurrection, so also being deeply moved to tears?

_____

_____

_____

_____

Evening: Do you find yourself able to accept that Jesus would weep with you over your losses even though he knows in time all your hurts will be healed? Or do you find yourself resisting the idea of Jesus weeping with you, and instead feeling that Jesus always pushing past emotions like grief or distress? Write out your answer.

_____

_____

_____

_____

_____

_____

_____

_____

By faith, imagine Jesus seeing your sorrow. Imagine him being deeply moved and troubled in spirit. Imagine him weeping with you and for you.

As you imagined that picture of Jesus, what affect did it have on you? On your relationship to Jesus? On your feelings toward God?

_____

_____

_____

_____

_____

_____

_____

DAY 3

Morning: Today's stride is to simply observe how others react to an expression of sadness on your part. How do people typically respond when you are honest about feeling sad or heavy-hearted? Today's stride is to simply observe this. Consider conducting a "social experiment".

When people ask how you're doing, say something such as, "I'm feeling sad today" or "I have a heavy heart right now." Take note of their reactions and how their reactions feel to you. If they ask in a genuine way about your sadness, you might say you're doing a study that's causing you to think more about your sadness and even tell a little of what your sadness is about. Again, observe their reactions, and how they feel to you.

Evening: Write your reflections about today's stride.

What was it like saying to others something such as, "I feel sad today"?

_____
_____
_____
_____
_____
_____
_____
_____
_____

How did most people respond?

_____
_____
_____
_____

What did their responses feel like to you?

_____
_____
_____
_____

Which response did you most appreciate?

_____
_____
_____
_____

Which response was most like what you would imagine Jesus would have?

_____

_____

_____

_____

_____

_____

How might you pray for those to whom you expressed your grief?

_____

_____

_____

_____

_____

DAY 4

Morning: In the New Living Translation, Galatians 6:2 reads, "Share each other's burdens, and in this way obey the law of Christ." Others can't share our burdens if we don't share our burdens with them. One reason we may not share our griefs with others is because we don't want to burden them. But if we keep our griefs to ourselves we can deprive others of an opportunity to fulfill Christ's way.

Another reason we may not share our griefs is that most people are not very good at handling them. They react awkwardly, change the subject, offer a pat answer rather than truly sharing the grief by feeling it with us and loving us in it.

A useful approach to overcoming this obstacle is to actually tell the person what you want when you share your heartache. Do you desire the person to simply listen without interrupting? Do you want her to weep with you? Do you want him to hold you? Do you want to be prayed for? Do you want direction or advice on what to do? James wrote, "You have not because you do not ask" (James 4:2 NASB).

This principle applies not just to our relationship with God but also our relationship with people. So today's stride is to:

1. Get in touch with your pocket of grief.

2. Ask yourself: What do I want or need, and from whom do I need it?

3. Sometime during the day, actually ask for what you want.
   For example, you might say something like: "I would like to share some of my heartache with you. I don't want you to fix it or even say anything. I just want to tell you how I feel and have you feel it with me. Would you be willing to do that?"

Evening: Write your reaction to today's stride:

_____
_____
_____
_____
_____
_____

Who did you choose to ask and why?

_____
_____
_____
_____
_____

How did you feel before approaching this person? What were your emotions and thoughts?

_____
_____
_____
_____
_____

What was it like telling the person your heartache and asking for what you wanted?

_____
_____
_____
_____
_____
_____

How did the person respond?

_____
_____
_____
_____
_____
_____

What did you feel and think afterwards?

_____
_____
_____
_____
_____
_____
_____

How do you find yourself praying for this person tonight?

_____
_____
_____
_____
_____
_____
_____

DAY 5

Morning: Today's stride is based upon Romans 12:15, "Rejoice with those that rejoice; mourn with those that mourn."

1. Keep an eye out for a person who appears to be distressed.

2. Approach the person and say something such as, "I get the sense you might be troubled today. I would like to hear about it if you would be willing to tell me."

3. If the person acknowledges some distress and tells you about it, simply try to feel what he or she is feeling. Sit with the person in the emotions for a few moments. Resist any urge to offer advice or even biblical assurances.

4. Thank the person for the honor of trusting you with something so precious as his or her pain. Tell the person you will keep him or her in your mind and prayers for the rest of the day.

Evening: What was it like for you to simply listen, to mourn with someone mourning, empathizing and resisting any urge to fix?

_____

_____

_____

_____

_____

_____

_____

How will you pray for this person?

_____

_____

_____

_____

_____

_____

_____

DAY 6

Morning: Read Genesis 39:1–20 in preparation for the next teaching episode. Write down anything that stands out to you.

_____
_____
_____
_____
_____
_____
_____
_____

See if you can think of a time when you did the right thing but you got punished for it in some way. Write the story below.

_____
_____
_____
_____
_____
_____
_____
_____
_____
_____
_____
_____
_____
_____
_____
_____
_____

Today, notice how you feel when you do something good or right, and yet are penalized for it in some way – in particular notice whether you feel more oneness with God and other Christians or more separation from God and other Christians.

Evening: What did you observe today about your reactions to being penalized for doing something good? Did you feel more alienated from God and his people, or more oneness with them?

_____

_____

_____

_____

_____

_____

What would it be like if, when you are repaid evil for good, you realized a great sense of solidarity and camaraderie with others who have experienced the same, with Joseph, Daniel, Paul and Jesus? What if when you received evil for good, you felt closer and more identified with Jesus and his people rather than more distant? What if you heard Jesus say to you, "I know, my child, I know. People did the same thing to me. Your unjust suffering is one more way that we are united."? How would that sense of union affect your reaction to the unfair treatment?

_____

_____

_____

_____

_____

_____

Close your day by slowly taking in the words of Matthew 5:10-12. Don't hurry. Let the words sink it. Note whatever significance you find.

_____

_____

_____

_____

_____

_____

Steve
PTSD

ACTS OF GOD

FAITHFUL UNDER TEMPTATION

ASSUME

EPISODE 3: FAITHFUL UNDER TEMPTATION

Joseph Loyalty to God

Notes from Small Group session:

Don't let your guard down

No matter the situation you are in, do your best

Finding Someone to Blame.
Friends & family ; prayers.

Joseph's Loyalty to God.

Our Father in heaven, hallowed be your name,
your kingdom come, your will be done, on earth as it is in heaven.
Give us today our daily bread.
And forgive us our debts, as we also have forgiven our debtors.
And lead us not into temptation, but deliver us from the evil one.
For yours is the kingdom and the power and the glory forever.
Amen.

DAILY STRIDES

DAY 1

Morning: This week you will work on becoming aware of the temptations that particularly try you during tough times. Think back to past struggles during times of despair or heartache. Check any below that apply.

During tough times, I am tempted to ...

☐ medicate the pain in some way—with food, prescription pills, TV, alcohol, or _____

☐ ignore the feeling; tell myself it doesn't exist, isn't real, or doesn't matter

☐ feel all alone, think everyone else is better off than me, wallow in self-pity, and remain a victim avoid life altogether and just sleep

☐ stop the sadness by becoming hard, callous, and invulnerable

☐ take control of everything around me—work, environment, people, even God—to limit my pain

☐ other _____
_____

As you go through your day, when you feel distressed or sad, just notice what temptation rushes in with an unhealthy answer.

Evening: Summarize your chief temptations when you are down.

Finding someone to blame
Friends, family
Praying
_____
_____
_____
_____

Try telling Jesus these temptations.

_____
_____
_____
_____
_____
_____
_____
_____

As you did so, what did you imagined to be Jesus' response? Does he...

____ shame you	or	____ understand you?
____ offer condemnation	or	____ offer forgiveness?
____ warn you never to do it again	or	____ recommend ways to deal with it?
____ leave it all up to you	or	____ promise help when you need it?

What story or passage from the Gospels would you offer to support the picture of Jesus that you just saw in your mind's eye?

_____

_____

_____

_____

_____

_____

_____

_____

_____

_____

Which version of Jesus, the one depicted in the left-hand column above, or the one depicted in the right-hand column, would be most likely to motivate to overcome temptations in difficult times, and why?

_____

_____

_____

_____

_____

_____

_____

_____

_____

_____

_____

_____

DAY 2

Morning: Today you will sort out whether what you have been calling "temptations" really are temptations or if they are simply natural needs during times of sadness. Feeling sad is human. Everyone, including Jesus, has felt deep sorrow and overwhelming distress. And there are natural needs in times of sorrow.

When the prophet Elijah was depressed and wanting to die, he pulled away from ministry, withdrew from contact with people, and simply slept. We're told in 1 Kings 19 that an angel appeared with food, telling him to eat. Then the angel allowed Elijah to sleep some more and then fed him again. Next, Elijah took a forty-day retreat into the wilderness to the mountain of God where he met the Lord in a deeper way and received insight into what to do next.

Were Elijah's withdrawal, sleeping, eating, and long sabbatical all sinful reactions to doubt, fear, and despair, when he should have toughed it out and remained in active ministry as a prophet? Or were those actions legitimate ways whereby he was healed of his heartache?

To cite another example, when in the Psalms David cried out to God expressing his anger and doubt, was this a legitimate way to work out his pain, or was his complaining a faithless act of sin?

When Paul was in prison, and he wrote to Timothy asking him to come see him, was this a reasonable need during distress, or was Paul falling into a temptation to rely on people rather than God?

When we face sadness and feel drawn to some reaction, we can ask ourselves some clarifying questions such as,

- Is this thing I desire to do a path toward healing or hiding?

- Is this an instrument by which I can recover, or is it something I use to simply numb myself and avoid the issue?

- Is this a way I can receive the grace of God, or is it a way I run from God?

Here is an example. After a major tragedy like the death of a child, would it be acceptable for a mother like Sarah to take a mild sedative for a period of time to help her sleep, or would that be evading the reality of the grief? A decision like this is a very personal one. A sedative could indeed be a way to get the needed rest to have the strength to then face the reality of the loss. But if the sedative came to be relied upon to avoid the pain, it may be a trap.

Look back over the ways you feel "tempted" to deal with your sadness. Are any of these "temptations" actually legitimate ways your body, mind, and spirit need to recover and heal? Write your thoughts below.

_____
_____
_____
_____
_____
_____
_____

Evening: Read 1 Kings 19:3-8, noticing in particular what the angel commands Elijah to do.

What might God be calling you to do in your grief that would help you recover but you've been denying because it feels ungodly, weak, faithless, or indulgent? Do you need more sleep? Would a period of solitude help? Is your soul crying out for a retreat? Could the pouring out of your honest feelings be cathartic? Do you need the comfort of a loving friend or counselor? What do your mind, body, and spirit require?

_____
_____
_____
_____
_____
_____

What will you do about these needs? Be specific.

_____

_____

_____

_____

_____

_____

_____

_____

_____

_____

_____

_____

_____

_____

_____

_____

DAY 3

Morning: Today's stride is to get in touch with your sorrow, find two ways of reacting to the pain, and observe what this is like.

First, think of a common temptation you face when discouraged or sad: alcohol, overeating, oversleeping, sexual fantasy, or something else. Write it here:

_____

Next, think of a healthy reaction you have discovered for grief: withdrawal to God, prayer, receiving comfort from a friend, crying, physical exercise, reading, or some other response:

_____

Consider these two options (the common temptation versus the healthy reaction) before you, and how they relate to dealing with grief and sadness. Look at the two paths. Feel the power and the call of each path. Observe the two paths without choosing either. Notice what they are saying to you, what they are promising you.

After pondering these two options, write what each is saying, what each is promising you. Describe their power and feel.

The unhealthy temptation says, promises, feels like …

_____

_____

_____

_____

_____

The healthy action says, promises, feels like …

_____

_____

_____

_____

_____

During this day, think back on your sadness, and when you do, notice these two options, again without choosing either.

Evening: Describe why you would or would not choose both options.

The unhealthy temptation:

Why I would choose it: _____

_____

_____

Why I wouldn't choose it: _____

_____

_____

The healthy reaction:

Why I would choose it: _____

_____

_____

Why I wouldn't choose it: _____

_____

_____

Choose one to act on now. Then write your reaction to taking that path.

_____

_____

_____

_____

_____

_____

Following this day's exercise, do you find more or less in agreement with what the Apostle Paul says in 1 Corinthians 10:13?

> *No temptation has overtaken you except*
> *what is common to mankind.*
> *And God is faithful; he will not let you be tempted*
> *beyond what you can bear.*
> *But when you are tempted, he will also provide*
> *a way out so that you can endure it.*

How do you find yourself praying now?

_____

_____

_____

_____

_____

_____

_____

DAY 4

Morning: Think about a specific time that you have been tempted. Take note of this in the space below.

_____

_____

_____

_____

_____

_____

As soon as many Christians feel tempted, they also feel as if God is distant, that he is already angry that they are harboring some ungodly desire. The result is that the tempted person feels alone in the temptation, as if it's up to them to overcome the attraction. If they succeed, they can then approach God with a report of success and feel good about themselves. If they fail, they feel they must withdraw from God for a period, as if they're in timeout or on probation. When sufficient time for remorse or self-reproach has occurred, they can again approach God and ask forgiveness.

Were you able to hold onto the sense that Jesus' loving, caring presence was still with you while you experienced temptation (in the example you wrote above)?

Some people believe that since Jesus is holy, he cannot remain with us when sin or even the temptation to sin is present. A verse commonly cited in support of this view is Habakkuk 1:13: "Your eyes are too pure to look on evil; you cannot tolerate wrongdoing." There are two problems with this view. The first is that if this were true, we would be left alone in our sin. If God cannot look on us or be with us when we are tempted or sinning, what hope of help do we have?

The second problem is that the whole Bible is a record of God indeed looking at and patiently tolerating wrongdoing. When we read the next lines in Habakkuk, we find that is exactly what God was doing, and exactly why Habakkuk was angry. God does allow evil. He continues to reach out to the wicked rather than quickly destroy them. The gospel message is that Jesus entered our rebellious world and became "a friend of tax collectors and sinners." The Pharisees were the ones who withdrew from sinful people; Jesus ate with them. He explained, "It is not the healthy who need a doctor, but the sick" (Mark 2:17). Paul assured us that wherever sin increases, grace increases all the more; that is, wherever there is sin, God is more, not less, present (Romans 5:20). The cross is the utmost expression of this truth. When man was at his worst, God was at his best. Christ not only tolerates our sin, but he became sin for us and, through him, God was reconciling the world to himself (2 Corinthians 5:19, 21).

Today's stride is to intentionally accept Christ's presence when you feel tempted to do wrong and to believe that Christ doesn't leave you when you do wrong. Hold on to this reality that when you are at your worst, Jesus is indeed at his best.

Evening: Think back over the course of your day. Were there any times that you were tempted to do wrong?

_____

_____

_____

_____

_____

Were you able to recall any of the morning's reading to help you sense Christ's presence in the midst of temptation?

_____

_____

_____

_____

_____

DAY 5

Morning: Today you will continue to practice the presence of Jesus not only in your sorrow but in your temptations. Your stride is to determinedly accept Jesus into your times of temptation—even if you succumb to the temptation—to hold onto your awareness of Jesus' presence, to allow him to "eat with you" even when you are a "tax collector and sinner."

Evening: What do you think of a holy Being who would stay even while being ignored, who will love even while being disobeyed, and who will not leave even when asked to do so? Write your thoughts.

_____

_____

_____

_____

_____

_____

DAY 6

Morning: Read Genesis 40 in preparation for the next teaching episode.

Note what Joseph said and did. Also indicate what you think those words and actions say about Joseph as a person.

What Joseph said and did	What that says about him
_____	_____
_____	_____
_____	_____
_____	_____
_____	_____
_____	_____

Joseph appears to not feel abandoned by God. The common wisdom of the day was that if terrible things happened to you, you were being punished by God. Why might Joseph have continued to hold to the belief that God was with him?

_____

_____

_____

_____

_____

If you were to be more like Joseph today, what might that look like?

_____

_____

_____

_____

_____

Are you willing to ask God for those character qualities?

_____

_____

_____

_____

_____

Evening: Read Genesis 40 as if for the first time. Imagine this story is totally new to you. Then notice your reaction to the last verse. Write your reaction below.

_____
_____
_____
_____
_____
_____
_____
_____
_____
_____

When in your life has the essence of this verse been true for you – that is, when have you had a series of setbacks and losses, then see what appears to be hope, only to have the hope cruelly disappointed? Tell the story here:

_____
_____
_____
_____
_____
_____
_____
_____
_____
_____
_____
_____
_____
_____
_____
_____
_____
_____
_____

Read the first line of Genesis 41. Do those words comfort you with a sense of, "I'm not the only one who has had to wait and wait and wait for relief," or do the words scare you with a fear of, "My troubles could go on much longer than I ever imagined"?

_____

_____

_____

_____

How did the story you told turn out – if it has turned out? What did it teach you?

_____

_____

_____

_____

_____

_____

_____

_____

_____

_____

_____

What do you find yourself saying to a God who will allow a good man like Joseph endure so much, and a person like you suffer the way you have?

_____

_____

_____

_____

_____

_____

_____

_____

_____

_____

_____

_____

ACTS OF GOD

FAITHFUL THROUGH ADVERSITY

EPISODE 4: FAITHFUL THROUGH ADVERSITY

Notes from Small Group session:

Denial

_____
_____
_____
_____
_____
_____
_____
_____
_____
_____
_____
_____
_____
_____
_____
_____
_____

David: What do you want?

Anna: I want to know when you're gonna go back to work. You know a lot of people depend on you there. So you're just gonna throw your life away?

David: Well, it's my life.

Anna: Is it?

David: No, it's God's life. That's the right answer, right? You know, because I haven't gone to Sunday school in a while so I'm just kind of a little rusty. What are you doing?

Anna: You feel that, David, a hundred thousand times a day through fifteen hundred miles of vessels, some as narrow as blood cells. How many times have I heard that one? Or the one about eyes and ears.

David: There are explanations.

Anna: You didn't believe any of them. You didn't believe it could all just come together. Not like...not like this. And then one bad thing, one terrible thing happens, and none of it matters anymore?

David: OK! OK! You win! You win! There is a God. There is God, and he is a monster.

Anna: David!

David: No, he's a monster. Think about it. What if it was me? What if it was me and I could heal Tracy and instead I just stood by and let her die? What if I could fix Becca but instead I just sat on hands and just let her slip away. What would you call me? What would you call me?

Anna: David, you're not God.

David: Get out. Get out! Get out!

|---|

Denial or avoidance   Recognition of
of the true extent   the true extent
of suffering   of suffering
in one's own life   in one's own life

|---|

Denial or avoidance   Recognition of
of the true extent   the true extent
of suffering   of suffering
in other's lives   in other's lives

DAILY STRIDES

During the next two weeks of Daily Strides we will wrestle more directly with the intellectual questions of suffering, so expect more reading and thinking than emotional work.

DAY 1

Morning: In the dialogue between David and Anna, her final statement was, "David, you're not God." Scripture makes clear that humans are not God, but Scripture also describes humans as made in the image of God. Read Genesis 1:26–27, below, and underline what is repeated for emphasis.

Then God said, "Let us make mankind in our image, in our likeness, so that they may rule over the fish in the sea and the birds in the sky, over the livestock and all the wild animals, and over all the creatures that move along the ground." So God created mankind in his own image, in the image of God he created them; male and female he created them.

In Psalm 8:3–5, two contrasting points are made about humanity.

When I consider Your heavens, the work of Your fingers,
  The moon and the stars, which You have ordained;
What is man that You take thought of him,
  And the son of man that You care for him?
Yet You have made him a little lower than God,
  And You crown him with glory and majesty!

(New American Standard Bible).

Another reference to the distance between God and humans is in Isaiah 40:13: "Who can fathom the Spirit of the Lord, or instruct the Lord as his counselor?" This verse could be taken to mean we are incapable of understanding God's ways at all. However, when Paul quoted this reference in two of his letters, he affirmed that we can indeed understand God's ways—and need to understand God's ways—though they are not instinctive to our fallen nature.

His first citation is found in Romans 11. In this letter Paul was conveying the idea that even though the Jewish people strived to be obedient to God, they had actually missed out on his grace; while the Gentiles, who did not try to be obedient, had been included in grace. The reason for this seemingly upside-down situation is that grace through Jesus is based in faith rather than on works of the law. In Romans 11:25, Paul wrote that he didn't want the Roman Christians to "be ignorant of this mystery." Notice that while what he described is a "mystery," it can also be known and grasped by ordinary people.

In verse 33, Paul cried out, "Oh, the depth of the riches of the wisdom and knowledge of God! How unsearchable his judgments, and his paths beyond tracing out!" Here is where he quoted Isaiah, "Who can fathom the Spirit of the Lord, or instruct the Lord as his counselor?" But his point was not that we can't understand what God is doing. Paul had just explained what God is doing! He is saving people on the basis of grace rather than works of law. His point was that the way God does things is not the way we naturally think God would act and not the way we would act if we were in charge of things.

Paul's second use of the Isaiah passage is in 1 Corinthians 2:12–16. Underline what stands out to you.

What we have received is not the spirit of the world, but the Spirit who is from God, so that we may understand what God has freely given us. This is what we speak, not in words taught us by human wisdom but in words taught by the Spirit, explaining spiritual realities with Spirit-taught words. The person without the Spirit does not accept the things that come from the Spirit of God but considers them foolishness, and cannot understand them because they are discerned only through the Spirit. The person with the Spirit makes judgments about all things, but such a person is not subject to merely human judgments, for, "Who has known the mind of the Lord so as to instruct him?" But we have the mind of Christ.

In these passages we find this both/and tension between God being infinitely greater than mankind yet mankind being sufficiently like God to understand God's ways in part. That's why Paul wrote in another place in this same letter,

For now we see only a reflection as in a mirror; then we shall see face to face. Now I know in part; then I shall be known fully, even as I am fully known (13:12).

While God's ways are not fully intelligible to us, neither are they so foreign or so high that we don't have a meaningful sense of them.

We will apply this principle to the problem of suffering, considering what about suffering is simply beyond our ability to grasp because we do not have God's intelligence and what part we can grasp but may not like because we do not have God's heart.

Tonight we will delve further into this issue. But for now, write your reactions to what you have read today.

_____
_____
_____
_____
_____
_____
_____
_____
_____
_____
_____
_____
_____

Evening: To continue the thoughts from this morning, you will be asked to face several series of dilemmas. As you respond, the underlying question will be if the issues are beyond your understanding or beyond your liking. The first series of questions relates to David's assertion that "a God who can save a child but doesn't is a monster."

Yes / No   If you had the godlike power to heal, would you heal every child on earth who was sick or injured so that none died?

If you circled no, respond to the questions in this box.

Describe your reasons for not stopping every child from dying.

_____

_____

_____

_____

_____

_____

_____

Would you consider yourself a monster for not stopping every child on earth from ever dying?

_____

_____

_____

_____

_____

_____

If you would not heal all children, would you heal at least some? If so, what criteria would you use for which children you would heal and which children you would not? Try to be specific. For example, you might say you would heal the children for whom people were praying. Then be more detailed. How many would have to pray? How much would they have to pray? How much faith would they have to have in their prayers being effective? Would the prayers have to come from Christians, or would you act on prayers from Jews, Muslims, Hindus, and other religious faiths? Would you make exceptions for orphans who had no one to pray for them?

_____

_____

_____

_____

_____

_____

If you circled yes, you would heal every child, respond to the questions in this box.

What would be the cutoff age at which a child would be allowed to die? Twenty-one? Eighteen? Twelve? Or would you prevent adults from dying as well? If so, what would be the cutoff age before death would be allowed? _____ years old

Let's say you set thirteen as the cutoff age before which no child was allowed to die. What would you say to the parents of a child who died on her fourteenth birthday when they ask why you couldn't have extended the cutoff a few hours or even made the cutoff fifteen?

_____
_____
_____
_____
_____
_____
_____
_____
_____

Now imagine yourself as a child who knows that no matter what you do, you cannot die. How would that change your decision making, risk taking, development, and obedience? What would be the upside and downside?

_____
_____
_____
_____
_____
_____
_____
_____
_____
_____

Now imagine yourself as the parent of a child who cannot die no matter what they do, you do, or anyone else does. What would be the consequences for how you parent?

_____

_____

_____

_____

_____

_____

_____

Would you be a better or worse parent?

_____

_____

_____

_____

_____

_____

_____

_____

_____

_____

Continue to mull over these questions. You might run them by family members, friends, or co-workers for their responses.

As you read through the questions, did you find yourself...

☐ diving into them, or
☐ giving up on them?

If you found yourself giving up, was it because the questions were...

☐ intellectually too hard—you couldn't really understand the concepts or issues, or
☐ emotionally too hard—you didn't like having to decide such important issues and feeling the weight of the ramifications?

How do you find yourself praying?

_____

_____

_____

_____

_____

_____

_____

_____

_____

_____

DAY 2

Morning: Today, again imagine yourself with godlike power to heal, and then respond to some very real-life questions. Yesterday you considered whether children should be allowed to die. But dying is not the only problem. Children also suffer pain without dying. Respond as best as you can to the following questions.

In medicine, a 10-point pain scale is often utilized. On this scale, what degree of pain would you allow in children? Circle your number.

0------1------2------3------4------5------6------7------8------9------10
No pain   Moderate   Worst possible

What percentage of the time would you allow a child to experience the level of pain you just circled? (For example, if you circled 5, would you allow a child to experience level 5 pain all the time or only a certain length of time?) _____% Explain your reasoning.

_____

_____

_____

_____

_____

_____

_____

Would you allow children who were more disobedient than others to experience a higher degree or duration of pain? If so, to what degree? Elaborate on your reasoning.

_____

_____

_____

_____

_____

_____

_____

_____

When you were a child, if you were able to experience only moderate pain no matter what you did, how would that have affected your development, decision-making, risk-taking, and obedience? What would be the upsides and downsides?

_____

_____

_____

_____

_____

_____

_____

_____

Imagine yourself as the parent of a child who could experience only moderate pain. How would that affect your parenting? Would you give more attention or less? How would you handle complaints? How about illnesses?

_____

_____

_____

_____

_____

_____

If you were able to stop death and limit pain to the degrees you decided in the questions above, do you think everyone would be content with your parameters and pleased with you? Why or why not?

_____

_____

_____

_____

_____

_____

_____

_____

_____

Continue to mull over these questions today. You might even ask family, friends, or co-workers for their responses.

Evening: As you continued to face these decisions, did you find yourself…

☐ still diving in, or

☐ throwing up your hands in exasperation?

If you found yourself giving up, is it because the questions are …

☐ more than you can think about, or

☐ more than you want to think about?

How do you find yourself praying after weighing all these questions?

_____

_____

_____

_____

_____

_____

_____

_____

_____

_____

DAY 3

Morning: Today's question is, if you could stop feeling pain, that is, shut down the neural network that communicates pain to the brain, would you choose to do so?

☐ No, I would leave my neural pain network unchanged, and continue to feel pain.

☐ Yes, I would disable my neural pain network so I never feel pain.

☐ Yes and no. I would modify my neural pain network in this way:

_____

_____

_____

_____

_____

In *Where Is God When It Hurts?* Phillip Yancey writes, "The pain network is easily the most unappreciated bodily system." He supports his assertion based on his association with Dr. Paul Brand, the highly acclaimed researcher on leprosy.

Brand spent decades working with leprosy patients. He discovered that the tissue damage common in leprosy sufferers was not due to some disease-caused degeneration but a secondary outcome. He found that lepers lose nerve sensation, beginning in their extremities. As a result of their inability to feel pressure and pain, they end up injuring themselves over and over, but without an awareness of the injuries. The gruesome result is the gradual loss of fingers, toes, and other body parts. Since they don't feel the pain, they lack either the awareness or motivation to prevent and treat their problems.

Yancey describes Brand's efforts to create a glove for lepers that would do what the nerve endings had stopped doing: communicate levels of sensation to the wearer. At first Brand attempted to design a pain-free system, but the low-level pressures proved too easy for patients to ignore. Brand tried buzzers and blinking lights, but still patients learned to disregard these signals. Finally the doctor had to resort to electric shocks, but patients would often simply stop using the glove, viewing it as an annoyance. Brand learned the system controls had to be out of a patient's reach; otherwise he would simply shut it down. Eventually, after five years and millions of dollars, his team abandoned the project as unfeasible.

Brand admitted that not all pain can be called good. "The one legitimate complaint you can make against pain is that it cannot be switched off. It can rage out of control, as with a terminal cancer patient, even though its warning has been heard and there is no more that can be done to treat the cause of the pain. But as a physician I'm sure that less than one percent of pain is in this category that we might call out of control. Ninety-nine percent of all the pains that people suffer are short-term pains: correctable situations that call for medication, rest, or a change in a person's lifestyle." Yet with this caveat, Brand's final conclusion was, "Thank God for inventing pain! I don't think he could have done a better job. It's beautiful."

What is your reaction to this reading? Jot your questions or thoughts.

_____

_____

_____

_____

_____

_____

_____

Read the above to someone else today, and ask for that person's reaction.

Evening: Look back at the questions for Day 3. Does today's reading change your answers in any way?

_____

_____

_____

_____

_____

_____

How are you led to pray?

_____

_____

_____

_____

_____

_____

_____

DAY 4

Morning: We continue to consider how God's ways and thoughts are higher than ours—whether they are simply indecipherable to us or just not to our liking. In Episode 1, this illustration was offered:

Even the most caring earthly father permits his children to experience pain to mature them and to prepare them for ultimate fulfillment and accomplishment. For example, when a dad takes the training wheels off the bicycle of his six-year-old child, he knows what's going to happen. A spill is inevitable, probably a painful scrape, maybe even bloodshed. But the father still takes the training wheels off and anx-iously watches from close-by because he knows that risk, adventure, and freedom are essential for his child's fulfilling life.

Today's questions are not as theoretical as those earlier this week. They explore the suffering you could prevent if you chose, but you allow.

If you are a parent, what suffering have you allowed (or caused) in your children that you could have prevented? If you are not a parent, respond in terms of another group over which you have had supervision, such as students, subordinates, or siblings. Brainstorm as many examples as possible in two minutes.

_____

_____

_____

_____

_____

_____

As you go through your day, think about the pains you allow others around you to suffer that you could prevent (a child struggling with homework when you could do the homework for her, a spouse doing dishes when you could do the dishes for him, a co-worker feeling pressured to find clients when you could find clients for her, another co-worker who is lonely that you could take to lunch, a neighbor staining his deck in the hot sun when you could do it for him, and so forth).

Evening: What did you observe today? How much do you let others suffer when you could prevent it?

_____
_____
_____
_____
_____
_____
_____

Why do you let others suffer when you can prevent the pain?

_____
_____
_____
_____
_____
_____
_____

When it comes to your children—or whatever group you chose to consider this morning—would you say they understand why you let them suffer as they have when it comes to things you could have prevented?

_____
_____
_____
_____
_____

How are you led to pray after considering these questions?

_____

_____

_____

_____

_____

_____

_____

_____

_____

DAY 5

Morning: Yesterday we considered how much suffering we allow others to endure that we could prevent and why we do so. Today we extend this question in a dramatic (and likely very uncomfortable) way. Right now there are orphaned children who need parents, hungry children who need food, and sick children who need medicine. You could prevent some of this suffering, but you consciously choose not to. Many of us could adopt orphaned children but we don't, not because we are incapable, but because it would be difficult and demanding. Many of us have extra money in the bank we are saving for a rainy day or retirement, while today is the rainy day for hungry children. You could feed and provide medicine to a few starving or sick children today. But you choose not to prevent this suffering that you could prevent.

The purpose here is not to create a guilt trip but to explore why we do not prevent suffering we could prevent. How do you respond to these challenging thoughts? Why don't you prevent more suffering than you do for orphaned, hungry, or sick children?

_____

_____

_____

_____

_____

_____

_____

_____

Again today, keep an eye out for suffering you could but choose not to prevent.

Evening: A common reply to this morning's questions is yes, I could help others more but it would be very hard, would take away from what my own family needs, and might endanger my own financial position. God, however, could feed them, clothe them, and give them parents without any hardship to himself. He could do it with a snap of his fingers.

If you have responded with something like the reasoning above, you need to consider the full implications of what you're saying. Let's grant that God could feed all the hungry children in the world without any strain. He doesn't, and that disturbs us. We wonder what kind of God lets children starve. But let's also grant that most of us could feed at least one more hungry child without any strain on our part. A child in many under-resourced countries can be fed for the price of a daily cup of coffee. You could feed a child with almost a snap of your fingers, with a few strokes on your computer keypad. But you don't. Someone might ask, "What kind of person are you that you would let a child starve when you could save him?" How would you respond?

_____
_____
_____
_____
_____
_____
_____
_____

We want to wiggle out of the logic presented above, but it's inescapable. Jesus warned us to be careful how we judge, "for in the same way you judge others, you will be judged, and with the measure you use, it will be measured to you" (Matthew 7:2). But we often judge God when it comes to the problem of suffering. We expect God to do what we don't do.

We can be like an assembly-line worker who complains that management doesn't care or else they would raise the pay, improve the benefits, and cut the hours. But when presented with the hard data that shows doing those things would cause layoffs or drive the company to bankruptcy, and then asked which actions he would take, the complainer responds with, "Don't ask me! I'm not in management. You can't expect me to figure out such things. If you really tried, you would find some way to raise our pay."

This line worker has a magical view of the economics of corporations. He is unwilling to face the realities of profit and loss, cause and effect. He is able to think only about himself.

In a similar way, we can have a magical view of God and creation. Why can't everyone just be well-paid, well-fed, well in body and mind? But we must be willing to face the cause-and-effect complexity of what we are asking.

Again, the purpose of these questions is not to trigger guilt. The purpose is to force us to consider the actual ramifications of our offhand judgments about what God should or shouldn't do. We find ourselves again faced with the question, Are God's ways beyond our understanding or beyond our liking?

Write your reaction to today's thoughts.

_____

_____

_____

_____

_____

How are you led to pray in light of all this?

_____

_____

_____

_____

_____

_____

DAY 6

Morning: Read Genesis 41, noting whatever stands out to you.

What questions come to mind upon reading this part of
Joseph's story?

_____
_____
_____
_____
_____
_____
_____
_____
_____
_____

Here are some difficult questions that arise from the segment of the
Joseph narrative. As you consider them, again notice whether you
sink your teeth into these tough questions or find yourself spitting
the questions out as too hard to chew on.

In v.32, Joseph states that the dream was given to Pharaoh twice
because it "firmly established,"(NIV), "decreed" (NLT), "fixed" (ESV),
"determined" (NASB) by God. As you read that verse, would it
imply to you that everything that happens is determined by God,
or only some things are determined by God and other events are
allowed to happen as circumstances and people determine?
Give your reasoning.

_____
_____
_____
_____
_____
_____
_____
_____
_____

If God firmly decides to orchestrate a lengthy famine, and as a result people starve to death, does that mean God is responsible for the deaths?

_____

_____

_____

_____

_____

_____

_____

How does it change your answer to the last question if God indeed orchestrates a famine, yet also forewarns of the famine, and provides several years of abundance in advance, so that people can prepare and not starve? Would these added factors affect your view of whether it is moral or immoral for God to intentionally bring about a famine?

_____

_____

_____

_____

_____

_____

_____

Some believers may respond to this week's line of questions with a statement of faith like this: "God is God and I'm not, so I don't question; I just accept it all on faith." What do you think of that perspective?

_____

_____

_____

_____

_____

_____

_____

How does the following example affect your response to the last question: If a person of Islamic persuasion said to you, "Allah is Allah and I'm not, so I don't question; I just accept it all on faith," would you allow that statement of faith as satisfactory and sufficient? Why or why not?

_____

_____

_____

_____

_____

_____

_____

_____

Joseph endured several years of slavery and prison, but came to a position of prominence and opulence. Would you be willing to following a similar road if it ended in a similar way? Why or why not?

_____

_____

_____

_____

_____

_____

_____

_____

Consider running these questions by some others today.

How do you find yourself praying after responding to these questions, and as you face your day?

_____

_____

_____

_____

_____

_____

_____

Evening: If you ran the questions from this morning by any others, what perspectives did you hear?

_____

_____

_____

_____

_____

_____

_____

_____

During this study, we have asked the question, what does faithfulness mean? Joseph is recognized as being faithful to God, yet in Genesis 41 we find him accommodating to Egyptian customs by shaving his head and beard, taking an Egyptian name, and marrying a foreign wife, the daughter of the high priest of a false god. These actions run contrary to the religious traditions of his fathers (though not to the Mosaic Law because it had not yet been given.) For example, Abraham made sure Isaac took a wife from among his people (Genesis 24); Isaac did the same with Jacob (Gen. 28:1). Now Joseph, the faithful one, marries an Egyptian woman. We might assume that Joseph had no choice or that he "converted" his wife to the worship of the God of his fathers, or that, even though he was a royal official, he never participated in the national religious life of the Egyptians. However the names of his two children provided in v. 45 mean respectively "she belongs to Neith" and "he whom Re hath given." Neith is an Egyptian goddess and Re is the sun god worshipped by the priests of On. All this raises some questions!

- Joseph obviously accommodated to the social and religious culture he found himself in. How much accommodation to the culture and the religion of those around us is acceptable before one might be considered to be "unfaithful?"

_____

_____

_____

_____

_____

• From the indications you see, did Joseph accommodate to his setting to the extent that violated the traditions and moral code handed down to him from his ancestors? If so, what would that mean?

_____

_____

_____

_____

_____

_____

• Does a person have to be perfectly correct in their all their beliefs about God or always choosing right in every faith decision in order to be considered faithful by God?

_____

_____

_____

_____

_____

As you read and consider these questions, how do they affect you? Do the questions and the struggle they provoke feel "faithful" to you, or does it feel "unfaithful" to wrestle in this way?

_____

_____

_____

_____

_____

_____

_____

_____

_____

_____

_____

_____

_____

_____

If wrestling in this way feels unfaithful, it may be helpful to know that Joseph's father, Jacob, received a second name from God. The name was "Israel," which became the primary moniker by which his descendants have been called ever after. He received this name after wrestling all night with a human manifestation of God (see Genesis 32). The name Israel means "one who struggles with God" and is given him because he wrestled with God and man and overcame.

The Judeo-Christian sacred history has always been one of wrestling with God, truth, and meaning. For further confirmation one only need scan Psalms, Job, Ecclesiastes, Jeremiah or Lamentations. God is portrayed as honoring not only faithfulness in terms of simple obedience, but at the same time honoring candid questions, honest struggles and sincere push back. Could it be that heartfelt wrestling with God about the meaning of suffering is a form of faithfulness?

How do you find yourself praying?

NOTES:

_____
_____
_____
_____
_____
_____
_____
_____
_____
_____
_____
_____
_____
_____
_____
_____
_____
_____
_____
_____
_____
_____
_____
_____
_____
_____
_____
_____
_____
_____
_____
_____
_____
_____
_____

FAITHFUL IN BLESSING

EPISODE 5: FAITHFUL IN BLESSING

Notes from Small Group session:

_____
_____
_____
_____
_____
_____
_____
_____
_____
_____
_____
_____
_____
_____
_____
_____
_____

*Command those who are rich in this present world not to be
arrogant nor to put their hope in wealth, which is so uncertain,
but to put their hope in God, who richly provides us with everything
for our enjoyment. Command them to do good, to be rich in good
deeds, and to be generous and willing to share. In this way they
will lay up treasure for themselves as a firm foundation for the
coming age, so that they may take hold of the life that is truly life*

(1 Timothy 6:17–19).

DAILY STRIDES

DAY 1

God-pleasing responses to prosperity:

☐ Embraced prosperity as an opportunity to glorify God
How: _____

_____

_____

☐ Served diligently for a prolonged period

How: _____

_____

_____

☐ Used position to benefit others

How: _____

_____

_____

Morning: At the gathering, you were asked to use the list above to check the ways you've responded during your greatest time of prosperity. Today, note some ways you are responding to your current degree of prosperity, whatever that may be.

Read the scripture printed on this week's Notes page out loud. *(Reading out loud often has a different effect than reading silently.)*

Choose one phrase from the passage upon which to focus today. Write it below. Command those who are rich in this present world not to be arrogant nor to put their hope in wealth, which is so uncertain, but to

Why this phrase? Put their hope in God, who richly provides us with everything for our enjoyment

Because I feel that people are too concerned with money & possessions, that they work their lives away & their families. They miss out on what God wants them to focus on, which is being obedient to him, not collecting things.

As you go through your day, notice how you handle your current degree of prosperity, and the extent to which it lines up with your chosen phrase.

Evening: What did you observe about how you tend to handle your level of prosperity?

_____
_____
_____
_____
_____

Would you say you are rich or prosperous?

PROSPEROUS   – flourishing
             – favourable or
                  promising

_____
_____

Ask God for his view. Would he say you are rich and prosperous? Write what comes to you.

_____
_____
_____
_____
_____

Take a few minutes to do an internet search on the phrase "wealth comparison calculator." Sites will pop up that include a comparison tool that allows you to see where you rank in affluence in relationship to the rest of the world. Sample two or three of the calculators and discover where they place your household. Write your reaction to what you find below.

I was surprised to learn that while I was @ 45% of the US annual wage, I earned 99% of the world average annual wage.

_____
_____
_____
_____

Re-read the scripture on the Notes page in light of what you discovered through the wealth comparison calculators. Does your take on this passage change in any way?

_____
_____
_____
_____
_____
_____
_____

How are you led to pray?

_____
_____
_____
_____
_____
_____
_____

DAY 2

Pitfalls:

☐ Felt superior just because I had more than others

How: _____
_____
_____

☐ Grew self-indulgent in disregard of others' needs

How: _____
_____
_____

☐ Developed a false security based on my prosperity

How: _____
_____
_____

☐ Became greedier rather than more generous

How: _____

_____

_____

☐ Ended up distracted from important and eternal things

How: _____

_____

_____

Morning: Which of the pitfalls are you still falling into?
Double check those.

Ask the Holy Spirit for his view on how you are doing with each
pitfall. Write what you sense below.

_____

_____

_____

_____

_____

_____

_____

_____

In Proverbs 30:8-9 we find this request, "Give me neither poverty
nor riches, but give me only my daily bread. Otherwise, I may have
too much and disown you and say, 'Who is the LORD?' Or I may
become poor and steal, and so dishonor the name of my God."
Is this a prayer you could echo? Why or why not?

_____

_____

_____

_____

_____

_____

_____

_____

When it comes to subjects of wealth and poverty, ease and hardship, how will you in fact pray? ?

_____
_____
_____
_____
_____
_____
_____
_____
_____
_____

Evening: Close this day with confession.

• Today I felt superior to others in this way:

_____
_____
_____
_____

• Today I was overindulgent in disregard to others' needs in this way:

_____
_____
_____
_____

• Today I experienced a false security in my belongings in this way:

_____
_____
_____
_____

• Today I was greedy for _____ in this way:

_____
_____
_____
_____

How do you feel now, as compared to before your confession?

_____

_____

_____

_____

_____

_____

_____

Do you believe you are forgiven "in accordance with the riches of God's grace" (Ephesians 1:7)? Why or why not?

_____

_____

_____

_____

_____

_____

_____

_____

DAY 3

Morning: Here is a part of the dialogue between Garrett and Bob:

Garrett: If there were a God, how could he let that little girl, Becca, die?
Bob: I don't know.
Garrett: Well, if you don't know, who does?
Bob: God.
Garrett: Thanks. That's helpful.
Bob: You want easy answers, but is that the way it works in your life, in your world? The really tough questions have easy answers? And as for why Becca Bradshaw is dead, I don't have the whole answer, but we both know that a part of the answer has something to do with you and the choices that you've made. Now maybe Sarah will forgive you, maybe not. But even if she does, will that bring you the peace that you're looking for?

What is your reaction to this dialogue?

_____

_____

_____

_____

_____

_____

_____

We see again the principle we have emphasized in this journal. Garrett may not have the answers to all the whys of suffering around him, and in particular in regards to Becca's death. But he does know a part of the why. And the part he does know, he doesn't like and wants to avoid.

The Times of London is said to have once sent out an inquiry to famous authors asking for essays as to what was wrong with the world. One reply simply read,

Dear Sir:

Regarding your question, "What is wrong with the world?"

I am.

Sincerely yours,
G. K. Chesterton

"I am the reason for suffering in the world" is not a complete answer to all suffering, but it's a part of the answer we avoid. If we aren't willing to see our part in the suffering of the world, can we ever hope to see clearly the other reasons? What do you think?

_____

_____

_____

_____

_____

_____

If you did have the complete answer as to why suffering happens, would that bring you the peace you are looking for? Why or why not?

_____

_____

_____

_____

_____

_____

_____

What keeps you from having peace today? Mull over this question as you carry out your activities today.

Evening: What would you need to have peace? What would it take? Try to be descriptive.

_____

_____

_____

_____

_____

_____

_____

_____

_____

How are you led to pray?

_____

_____

_____

_____

_____

_____

_____

_____

DAY 4

Morning: In this section of the Traveler's Journal we have turned our focus on some of the tough questions about suffering. Now we face a dilemma that again calls for the acceptance of complexity over simplicity, embracing a way we may not like but is not completely beyond our understanding.

In Matthew 17:20, Jesus' disciples found themselves unable to heal a demon-possessed boy and asked Jesus about it. He famously replied,

Because you have so little faith. Truly I tell you, if you have faith as small as a mustard seed, you can say to this mountain, "Move from here to there," and it will move. Nothing will be impossible for you.

A similar saying is found in Mark 11 after Jesus cursed a fig tree and the disciples found it withered. Jesus said in verses 23–24,

Truly I tell you, if anyone says to this mountain, "Go, throw yourself into the sea," and does not doubt in their heart but believes that what they say will happen, it will be done for them. Therefore I tell you, whatever you ask for in prayer, believe that you have received it, and it will be yours.

These promises seem clear and simple. Many people take the promises as a blank check that can be cashed at any time for almost anything, as long as they can muster sufficient faith, and not doubt. But when the child is not healed, the cancer does not regress, or a baby is not conceived, many people conclude either,

A. We didn't have enough faith; it's our fault, or

B. Jesus' word can't be trusted; it's God's fault.

But a third option exists. This option arises when we remember that God's ways and thoughts are not like our ways and thoughts. His ways are more complex than we usually like but not necessarily more obscure than we can understand. We prefer things to be simple: Jesus said it. I believe it. That settles it. But we can't just look at one passage to the exclusion of all the others. For example, not all of Jesus' prayers were answered in the affirmative. Consider Matthew 26:39, in which Jesus prayed in the Garden of Gethsemane:

"My Father, if it is possible, may this cup be taken from me."

Hold it! In Matthew 17:20, Jesus said nothing will be impossible for those with as little as a mustard seed of faith. Believers can even move mountains. But in Matthew 26:39, Jesus said, "if it is possible" (the same Greek root word for possible is used). If nothing is impossible, why did Jesus say, "if it is possible"? Did Jesus forget what he had said earlier? Did Jesus not have enough faith to move the mountain called Calvary? Did Jesus give into doubt in the garden? How would you respond to someone with these questions?

_____

_____

_____

_____

_____

_____

_____

_____

_____

Do you find yourself throwing up your arms in exasperation, screaming, "I don't know! Just give me the answer!"? If so, is it because you can't think about these questions or because you don't want to think about them? We can be like Garrett Connors in that we want a simple, easy answer from the preacher, from the Bible, from Jesus. But is life simple? Are the physics of the universe simple? Is the biology of living creatures simple? Is the anatomy and functionality of the human brain and body simple? Are the ways people and cultures form and interact simple?

This is one of the many respects in which God's ways are different from ours: we want simple and easy—no strain, no fuss, no mess—while life tends to be complex, difficult, and full of mystery.

Tonight we'll look further at today's dilemma. But for now, turn this question over in your mind. Why would Jesus say nothing is impossible for those who believe, and then pray asking if escape from the cross were possible? You may even present the dilemma to others for their response.

Evening: We continue work from this morning, asking why Jesus would say all things are possible to those who believe, even the moving of mountains, and then ask the Father if it were possible to evade the mountain called Calvary. Why couldn't he believe that he had already received a reprieve from that suffering, and then be sure he had it?

One answer has to do with a little Greek word, **dei** (pronounced "day"), which is usually translated "it is necessary." According to Thayer's Greek Lexicon, something may be "necessary" because,

- the necessity lies in a thing's very nature
- the necessity is due to circumstances
- the necessity must occur to attain some end
- the necessity is a law, command, or duty
- the necessity is a decree of God

Ten times in the Gospels we are told that it was necessary for Jesus to suffer and be put to death. Jesus himself said it, after Peter confessed Jesus as the Christ for the first time.

From then on Jesus began to tell his disciples plainly that it was necessary (dei) for him to go to Jerusalem, and that he would suffer many terrible things at the hands of the elders, the leading priests, and the teachers of religious law. He would be killed, but on the third day he would be raised from the dead

(Matthew 16:21, NLT).

So we see this tension:

- Some things are necessary to be as they are; they either cannot or should not be changed; they may even be impossible to change for some important reason.
- Some things are not necessary to be as they are and so may be changed through prayer or action.

Why would Jesus say words like, "nothing will be impossible for you" or "whatever you ask for in prayer, believe that you have received it, and it will be yours," if this isn't really the case, if there are indeed things that cannot be changed?

To answer, here is another thought question. Imagine you say to your child (or niece or nephew), "I promise we will go to the zoo Saturday if you ask nicely," and the child does ask nicely. Are there any factors that might lead you to not keep your promise? For example, would you still go to the zoo if,

☐ the child is sick with the flu and running a temperature of 103 degrees?

☐ the child is disobedient all week long: sassing, breaking things, hitting his siblings, refusing to do homework?

☐ your mother dies and the funeral is Saturday?

☐ the zoo is closed due to a gas leak?

How does this example affect your interpretation of Jesus' promise that we can receive whatever we ask for in faith?

_____

_____

_____

_____

_____

_____

_____

_____

_____

_____

Look over the list of extenuating circumstances that could cause you to "break your word." In each case, what would you say to the child who protests, "But you promised. Didn't I ask nicely enough? Don't you love me? Were you lying when you said we would go to the zoo?"

How are you led to pray to your Father in heaven?

DAY 5

Morning/Evening: Today we look at two other passages that relate to the question of suffering where the Greek word dei is used. The first is Acts 14:22, in which Paul and Barnabas told their new converts,

We must (dei) go through many hardships to enter the kingdom of God.

The second is 1 Peter 1:6:

There is wonderful joy ahead, even though you have to (dei) endure many trials for a little while (NLT).

These two passages assure that trials are a necessary, inescapable part of what will happen to believers. Someone might protest, "But if I prayed correctly and with enough faith, couldn't these hardships and trials be moved like mountains and thrown into the sea? Didn't Paul, Barnabas, and Peter know what Jesus said about believing and receiving if one has enough faith, that anything is possible for those who don't doubt?"

Of course they knew those sayings. But they also knew life—and God—is a little more complex than any one verse can disclose. In the next paragraph, Peter gave us one reason why trials are necessary, a reason no amount of prayer can undo:

These trials will show that your faith is genuine. It is being tested as fire tests and purifies gold—though your faith is far more precious than mere gold. So when your faith remains strong through many trials, it will bring you much praise and glory and honor on the day when Jesus Christ is revealed to the whole world (1 Peter 1:7, NLT).

Here we see one reason (or two or three reasons) for the necessity of trials—that faith may be tested, then purified, and ultimately bring us praise, glory, and honor. We might be tempted to say, "Oh, here is the reason for all trials. All trials are necessary tests of faith." But again this would be oversimplifying the issue. The Scripture is much more multifaceted. Peter was giving just one general reason trials are necessary.

In 2 Corinthians 12 we see another possible reason for necessary suffering. Paul wrote about his experience of a thorn in the flesh, "a messenger of Satan, to torment me" (v. 7). He said this thorn was "given" to him, and he provided the reason: to prevent him from becoming conceited. But couldn't he pray this satanic messenger away if he had enough faith and didn't doubt? Apparently not. He wrote, "Three times I pleaded with the Lord to take it away from me" (v. 8). He received this answer: "My grace is sufficient for you, for my power is made perfect in weakness."

"Therefore," Paul said, "I will boast all the more gladly about my weaknesses, so that Christ's power may rest on me."

Does this mean every trial we suffer is a messenger of Satan to keep us humble? Not at all. In chapter 1 of this same letter, Paul gave two other reasons for his suffering. In verse 6 he said that some of his sufferings were actually for the comfort and salvation of other believers. Then he went on to describe "troubles" and "great pressure, far beyond our ability to endure" that he and his companions had recently faced. It was so bad that they "despaired of life itself." The purpose he found in these hardships is given in verse 9:

"This happened that we might not rely on ourselves but on God, who raises the dead."

So we have found two more possible reasons for adversity: so others can be blessed and we might not rely wholly on ourselves. Does that exhaust all the possible reasons suffering happens? Again, no! The New Testament attributes suffering to disease, evil spirits, the freewill decisions of other people, our own freewill decisions, God's discipline, and the natural consequences of living in a real world with established natural laws. All these aspects of the created order have their own "necessity."

When we give over-simplified answers to questions such as why there's so much suffering in the world or why that little girl died in the car wreck, we're not moving closer to truth but further away.

A prime example is found in John 9:

As Jesus went along, he saw a man blind from birth. His disciples asked him, "Rabbi, who sinned, this man or his parents, that he was born blind?" (vv. 1–2).

Note the simplistic perspective. Why is this man suffering? Only two possible causes were even entertained. Either this man sinned to bring on his blindness, or his parents' sin led to his blindness. This narrow, cut-and-dry perspective is so human. People want to find easy, unambiguous reasons for things, and, if possible, blame someone else in the process. But this is not God's way. Jesus responded,

Neither this man nor his parents sinned ... but this happened so that the works of God might be displayed in him. As long as it is day, we must do the works of him who sent me (vv. 3–4).

Instead of providing the "real" reason why this man was suffering, Jesus asserted what our response to suffering ought to be. Our response shouldn't be to sit back and piously figure out why the suffering has happened. Rather, it should be to do the work of God in the midst of the suffering—to serve, to engage, to help. This moves us from being passive observers and judges (very human), to being active helpers and healers (very divine).

Yes, we can know some general reasons why suffering occurs. But we cannot know the full reason why any specific incident of suffering occurs. That is why in a similar passage Jesus said,

And what about the eighteen people who died when the tower in Siloam fell on them? Were they the worst sinners in Jerusalem? (Luke 13:4, NLT).

The typical answer of his day would have been yes, these men must have done something particularly offensive to have this happen to them. But Jesus' answer was, "I tell you, no! But unless you repent, you too will all perish" (v. 5, New International Version). Notice that

Jesus directed the focus away from the natural human tendency to judge why something happened and turned it toward something we can do in light of suffering. In this case, what we can do is turn away from our own sin to avoid its assured consequences.

Conclusions:
1. The reasons for suffering are many and complex.

2. While I can understand some of the reasons why suffering occurs—they are not totally obscure to me—I cannot know all the reasons.

3. While I can understand some of the reasons why a particular episode of suffering occurs, I cannot know all the reasons. To make a cut-and-dry judgment about why a particular episode of suffering happened is not to move closer to truth but further away.

4. Some of the reasons suffering occurs have to do with me and my actions. To fail to see this reality will hinder me from seeing clearly at all.

5. My most godly response to suffering is not to judge the reasons for it, but to have compassion toward the sufferers and alleviate the suffering if possible. This is what Jesus did and urges me to do.

What are your feelings and thoughts in response to this reading and the points made above? Can you summarize it in your own words?

_____
_____
_____
_____
_____
_____
_____
_____
_____
_____
_____
_____
_____
_____

DAY 6

Morning: Read Genesis 41:56—45:15 and 50:15–21. This is a long section, so read it like you would any "normal" story, that is, take the ride, feel the twists and turns, notice your reactions.

Note what stood out to you.

_____
_____
_____
_____
_____
_____
_____
_____
_____
_____
_____

Do you find the story to be simple, clear, and straightforward, or do you find the story to be complex, a bit cloudy, with a healthy degree of ambiguity?

_____
_____
_____
_____
_____
_____
_____
_____

The prevalence and effects of deception is a repeated theme not just in Joseph's story but in the whole Genesis narrative.

- Adam and Eve are deceived by the serpent, losing their place in paradise.

- Abraham is called to be a man through whom "all peoples on earth will be blessed" yet ten verses into his story we find him plotting a deception (Genesis 12:10-13).

- Abraham's promised son Isaac repeats his father's ruse (Genesis 26).

- Deception increases with Abraham's grandson, Jacob, whose very name denotes trickery. Jacob hoodwinked his own father and so stole his brother Esau's rightful blessing.

- The trickster is tricked himself when Jacob is deceived by his uncle Laban, who fooled him into marrying a different daughter than promised, and so forced Jacob to work an extra seven years for the wife he really wanted. Jacob and Laban continued attempts to swindle the other until they finally parted in a strained peace.

- When we come to the Joseph narrative, we find Jacob who exemplified trickery again being deceived. Just as he conned his father, his sons lie to him regarding the fate of his favored child, Joseph.

- In today's section of scripture, who does the deceiving, and why?

_____

_____

_____

_____

_____

_____

Here again we find Joseph, the faithful one, doing and saying things that could be considered shady at best and outright dishonest at worst. He not only passively deceives his brothers but directly lies more than once. However, Joseph's deception is not committed in order to benefit himself, but to test his brothers' words. Do you find Joseph's deception morally objectionable or justifiable considering the circumstances?

_____

_____

_____

_____

_____

_____

Interestingly, the conniving continues, even after the reconciliation. Following Jacob's death, the ten brothers feared Joseph would now execute them for their crime. So they fabricated a lie about what Jacob said before his death. This theme of deception continued throughout the biblical narrative, and culminated when the favored Son of Heavenly Father was betrayed by Judas' deceptive kiss, slandered by false witnesses and disowned by Peter's denial.

Yet we find again, what humans intend for evil, God transforms into good. Humanity's dishonest behavior is used for humanity's deliverance. Could it be that the only one who can be said to be completely faithful in Joseph's story, and in any story, is God himself?

What if some were unfaithful? Will their unfaithfulness nullify God's faithfulness?

Not at all! Let God be true, and every human being a liar. (Romans 3:3-4)

What would it be like to live this day with the firm conviction that, even if every other person you meet is untrue and untrustworthy, and even if I fail and an unfaithful, that God will remain faithful, working all things for good?

_____
_____
_____
_____
_____
_____

Try living today with that conviction at the forefront of your mind.

_____
_____
_____
_____
_____
_____
_____

Evening: Genesis 50:20 contains the heart of the Joseph story. Read the verse again.

What do you think Joseph meant? Was Joseph implying that...

☐ God caused his brothers to hate him, attack him, and sell him into slavery?

☐ God took the raw material of his brothers' choices and skillfully worked that evil into surprising and surpassing good, in this case, the saving of his family?

Express your reasoning.

_____

_____

_____

_____

_____

_____

_____

_____

_____

_____

Look up and read Romans 8:28. Like Genesis 50:20, this verse makes it clear that God is working in everything for good. But exactly how God is doing so is not so clear. Read the remainder of Romans 8 and notice what Paul says cannot stop God from working good.

The crucifixion of Jesus conveys many messages. One of those messages is that the very worst thing man can do is never so powerful that God cannot make something beautiful out of it. In Jesus' death , man committed the most heinous act possible – deicide, the murder of deity. Yet out of this lowest possible action, God orchestrates the greatest ever good, "the saving of many lives," even the salvation of humankind.

Which God is greater?

☐ A God who controls everything so that nothing bad or painful ever happens

☐ A God who allows real agents their freedom, and out of that freedom, even when it is abused, creates even greater good

Express the reasons for your choice.

_____

_____

_____

_____

_____

_____

_____

_____

_____

_____

What good is God working for us? According to Romans 8, not just the saving our physical lives, but the conforming of our natures into the image of his Son, that is, to give us the life that truly is life. This is not just mere biological life, but eternal life, the quality of life that Jesus himself has with the Father. Would this end be worth the suffering involved in getting there?

_____

_____

_____

_____

_____

_____

_____

_____

_____

_____

_____

_____

NOTES:

ACTS OF GOD

PURPOSE OF PAIN

EPISODE 6: PURPOSE OF PAIN

Notes from Small Group session:

_____
_____
_____
_____
_____
_____
_____
_____
_____
_____
_____
_____
_____
_____
_____
_____

Sarah's courtroom speech:

I've been thinking about what I would say today for months. I wrote it down so I wouldn't leave anything out. All of this is because of that little girl right there. My little girl. That girl was so full of love and joy. Sometimes it blinded me just to look at her. The day that photo was taken, I told her, her socks didn't match and she said, "Yes they do, Mommy. The purple one matches my personality and the white one matches my eyeball."

There is no punishment that would fit the crime of destroying that little girl. Not one hundred years in a cage or hanging or a firing squad or a guillotine. Garrett Connors got drunk, ran a red light, and smashed into my car, and because of it Becca is dead.

I've asked myself a million times, if there is a God, a good God, why is Becca dead? Because there is a good God, Becca is not dead. But what if it's real? What if he wiped away all the tears? Becca is alive. She's beautiful and joyful.

I believe that. I know it's true but I can't have it both ways. I can't believe that God is caring for my little girl in heaven; I can't know that in my heart if my heart's full of fight and hatred and revenge.

I forgive you.

It's not easy. It's the hardest thing I've ever done. It's not a one-time thing either. I did it today. I'll get up tomorrow morning and I'll do it again. A God powerful enough to create a beautiful place for Becca and Blake and me is powerful enough to give me the strength to forgive again and again as long as it takes.

Please show mercy and compassion to this man. Revenge won't bring Becca back. It will only stain her passing and make it ugly and despairing. I want what happens today in the courtroom to be light, not darkness, a moment of pure grace. That alone will be a fitting memorial to the life of Rebecca Anne Bradshaw.

Three ways forgiveness is portrayed in this episode:

A. Joseph forgave but only after he had tested his brothers to see if they had changed. It seems he forgave because his brothers had matured and because he saw the good that came out of their evil actions.

B. Sarah forgave not because of any change she saw in Jarrod Connors or because she saw any good come from Becca's death. She forgave because she couldn't hold onto bitterness and at the same time believe that a loving God was caring for Becca.

C. Jesus said from the cross, "Father, forgive them for they do not know what they are doing" (Luke 23:34). He didn't forgive because of some change in people or because of the good he saw coming from evil, though he did see good coming from the evil done to him. Rather, he forgave because he is forgiveness. Being in very nature God, he displayed what God's character is like. God is love. God is forgiveness. Jesus loved and forgave because that is who he is, not because of any exterior reason.

And we know that in all things God works for the good of those who love him, who have been called according to his purpose

(Romans 8:28).

Participant's Feedback: If your group is not proceeding to the Traveling Beyond section, tell us about your experience of the main study. We value your comments! Send your comments to info@cityonahillstudio.com

INTRODUCTION TO TRAVELING BEYOND

This study includes bonus material called "Traveling Beyond: A Healing Journey" available for free via pdf by emailing info@cityonahillstudio.com. This part of the study is "beyond" not just because it goes beyond the given timeframe of the video study, but it also goes beyond the normal parameters of a Bible study.

The purpose of the Traveling Beyond material is to guide group members through a practical process of working through one experience of suffering in their own lives, while at the same time recollecting and celebrating one cheerful episode in their lives. Traveling Beyond includes direction in:

- making a timeline of your life: the primary positive and primary negative experiences and sharing this timeline with the group (or a subset of the group)
- choosing one positive and one negative life experience to work through in greater detail and creating a timeline for both experiences
- sharing these timelines with the group (or a subset of the group)
- working through a cluster of reflections regarding the one positive and one negative experience then sharing those reflections
- formulating a letter to God about both the positive and negative events; this letter will resemble a personal psalm
- reading this letter to the group (or a subset of the group)

WHY DO TRAVELING BEYOND?

1. It provides a practical way to work through and make the most of the good and bad of life.

When people find themselves severely challenged by the traumas of life, they can either:

A. get stuck in their hurts, unable to get out, and end up being defined by their tragedies, or

B. try to ignore their hurts—saying things like: It is what it is. Why cry over spilled milk? You can't change the past, so why dwell on it?— and end up detached from their emotions and the feelings of others.

A better way is to work through both our gains and our losses, learning from them, allowing them to develop empathy, character, and wisdom in us. After all, the bad things have already happened! In a sense, we have already paid our tuition fees to the School of Suffering. Why not derive as much meaning and value out of our troubles as we can?

2. Many people don't know what to do with their heartaches or how to work through them. Often, those around them don't understand and don't want to hear about it. So people can feel alone in their grief with no structured way to work through it.

Traveling Beyond provides one sensible, concrete method for working through heartache. It is not the only way. But it is a helpful way. After following this method once, a person has a practical way to work through future losses (and likely there will be future losses).

3. Doing Traveling Beyond has the power to bond our small group in a deep and profound way. When we share our deepest joys and sorrows—and not just in a general "prayer request" fashion such as "I'm having a hard time at work" or "I'm sad since my dad died," but in a specific, detailed manner—we connect at the most personal level. We go further in experiencing Galatians 6:2, carrying each other's burdens and so fulfilling the law of Christ.

If the group is to get the most out of Traveling Beyond, everyone should agree to participate in the sharing. This sharing may be with the whole group or with a smaller subset of the group, as the group chooses. The agreement of all to share is important because if some choose not to, then those who do share may feel like (or feel silently labeled as) the "needy ones" or "the weak ones." Also, those who don't share can be tempted to maintain a misleading sense of self-sufficiency or invulnerability.

We suggest group members deliberate about doing Traveling Beyond until the next gathering. During that time, members can look through the Traveling Beyond section of the Traveler's Journal to get a sense of what it's like. Also, the journal provides direction on coming to one's own conclusion.

The time duration for Traveling Beyond depends on the size of the group and the decision about whether or not to divide into subsets. The minimum length is six gatherings, including the decision-making gathering.

DAILY STRIDES

The purpose of this week's Daily Strides is to facilitate your thinking regarding Traveling Beyond.

DAY 1

Morning: Reread the introduction to Traveling Beyond. Jot your immediate reaction below.

_____

_____

_____

_____

_____

Paul wrote in Ephesians 5:15-16, "Be very careful, then, how you live--not as unwise but as wise, making the most of every opportunity, because the days are evil."

Does pursuing Traveling Beyond appear to you to be wise or unwise? Express your reasoning.

_____

_____

_____

_____

_____

_____

Does Traveling Beyond appear to you as an opportunity to learn from your past hurts and help others in their struggles or does it appear more likely your group would be wasting time that could be better spent on something else?

_____

_____

_____

_____

_____

_____

Do you think Traveling Beyond would help you face the "evil days" we live in (Ephesians 5:15-16), or would it would it somehow make you more susceptible to the evil days around you?

_____

_____

_____

_____

_____

_____

Talk to God about how you might live out Ephesians 5:15-16 today.

_____

_____

_____

_____

_____

_____

Evening: Go back to the Feelings Chart on page 32. Which emotions do you experience when thinking about doing Traveling Beyond?

Emotion   Thought

_____ | _____
                 | _____
_____ | _____
                 | _____
_____ | _____
                 | _____
_____ | _____
                 | _____
_____ | _____

Attach a thought to each of the emotions you just listed. For example, you might write something like, "Excited… because I am hopeful this will break me out of a stuck place" or "Anxious… because this might be more painful than I can endure."

Do these emotions and thoughts lead you to be more or less likely to do Traveling Beyond?

_____
_____
_____
_____

Express these emotions and thoughts to Jesus.

_____
_____
_____
_____
_____
_____
_____
_____
_____
_____

DAY 2

Morning: "The one who states his case first seems right, until the other comes and examines him" (Proverbs 18:17, ESV). Today, take both sides.

What are the negatives of doing Traveling Beyond? List as many as you can think of.

_____
_____
_____
_____
_____
_____
_____

What are the positives of doing Traveling Beyond? List as many as you can think of.

_____
_____
_____
_____
_____
_____
_____

See if any others come to you during the day.

Evening: Circle the two or three greatest negatives and greatest positives.

What do these positives and negatives say to you regarding Traveling Beyond?

_____
_____
_____
_____
_____

How are you led to pray?

_____

_____

_____

_____

_____

_____

DAY 3

Morning: "I applied my heart to what I observed and learned a lesson from what I saw" (Proverbs 24:32).

Are you acquainted with anyone who has worked through a program similar to Traveling Beyond? If so, what do you learn from their experience?

_____

_____

_____

_____

_____

_____

Have you ever done anything like what is suggested in Traveling Beyond? If so, what was it like? If not, what do you imagine it would be like?

_____

_____

_____

_____

_____

_____

_____

_____

Ask God for what you need for this day.

Evening: Think of one person in the group, whoever comes to mind first.

What do you imagine it would be like for this person to work through Traveling Beyond? Jot some thoughts.

_____
_____
_____
_____
_____
_____
_____
_____

Do your thoughts lead you to desire or not desire that this person work through the material?

_____
_____
_____
_____
_____
_____
_____
_____

How will you pray for this person?

_____
_____
_____
_____
_____
_____
_____
_____
_____
_____

DAY 4

Morning: "We are many parts of one body, and we all belong to each other" (Romans 12:5 NLT).

Think about the group as a whole. What would you say are the strengths and weaknesses of your small group?

Strengths	Weaknesses
_____	_____
_____	_____
_____	_____
_____	_____
_____	_____
_____	_____
_____	_____

For what are you most grateful in this group? Express that to Jesus.

_____

_____

_____

_____

_____

_____

_____

_____

Evening: Considering the strengths and weaknesses of the group, would doing Traveling Beyond be beneficial or non-beneficial? Express your thinking.

_____

_____

_____

_____

_____

What will you pray for your group?

_____

_____

_____

_____

_____

_____

_____

_____

DAY 5

Morning: "For by the grace given me I say to every one of you: Do not think of yourself more highly than you ought, but rather think of yourself with sober judgment, in accordance with the faith God has distributed to each of you" (Romans 12:3).

What are your greatest strengths and weaknesses at this point in your development as a human being?

Strengths	Weaknesses

What strength or weakness would you like to focus on today?

_____

_____

_____

_____

_____

_____

Evening: Considering your strengths and weaknesses, would doing Traveling Beyond be beneficial or non-beneficial? Express your thinking.

_____
_____
_____
_____
_____
_____
_____

What will you pray for yourself?

_____
_____
_____
_____
_____
_____

DAY 6

Morning: "If you need wisdom, ask our generous God, and he will give it to you. He will not rebuke you for asking" (James 1:5NLT).

Ask the Father for his direction on your small group doing Traveling Beyond. Be open to what he says to you right now and what he says to you throughout your day.

Evening: What do you sense God saying to you?

_____
_____
_____
_____
_____
_____
_____
_____

If you don't have a sense of how God is leading you, consider two reasons James provides in 1:6-8 and 4:3 for why we may not receive an answer to our request for wisdom. Do either of these reasons connect to you?

_____

_____

_____

_____

_____

_____

_____

As this journal has often repeated, the reasons for anything are complex rather than simple. So the reason(s) you may not receive immediate wisdom from God on this question today may have nothing to do with lacking faith or having selfish motives. If you don't have a sense of direction from the Holy Spirit, what conclusion do you come to based on your experience and Scripture?

_____

_____

_____

_____

_____

_____

_____

_____

_____

What are you led to pray?

_____

_____

_____

_____

_____

_____

DAY 7

Morning: Take a Sabbath from all your thinking. Choose something utterly frivolous to do, something you enjoy but with no "productive" value. Choosing to do something frivolous and enjoyable can be an act of faith. It affirms that you are not God, that the destiny of the universe is not up to you, that God loves you and wants more for you than just work.

Evening: What enjoyable yet frivolous activity did you choose?

_____
_____
_____
_____
_____
_____
_____

How did you feel while doing it?

_____
_____
_____
_____
_____
_____

Tell Jesus about it, like you would tell a friend.

What do you sense is his reaction?

_____
_____
_____
_____
_____
_____
_____

To receive the remainder of "Traveling Beyond" free via pdf, email info@cityonahillstudio.com

NOTES:

NOTES:

NOTES:

NOTES:

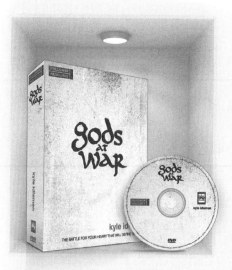

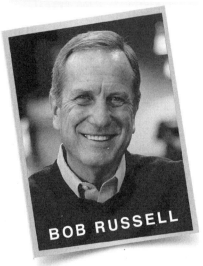

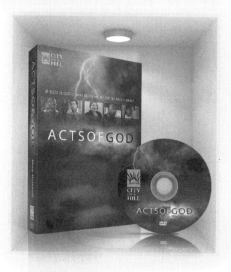